Enchantment

of The Witch's Art
of Manipulation through
Gesture, Gaze and Glammour

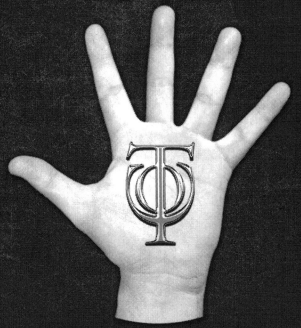

Peter Paddon

Enchantment

of The Witch's Art
of Manipulation through
Gesture, Gaze and Glamour

Peter Paddon

PENDRAIG Publishing
Los Angeles, CA 91040

Enchantment
The Witch's Art of Manipulation Through Gesture, Gaze and Glamour
by Peter Paddon
First Edition © 2013
by PENDRAIG Publishing

Cover Design & Interior Images
Typeset & Layout   Jo-Ann Byers Mierzwicki

Transcription of workshops by   Glenda Chism Tamblyn
Photographs by   Linda and Peter Paddon
Photographic models: Christopher Michael and
                                    Anna Strongwolf

PENDRAIG

PENDRAIG Publishing
Los Angeles, CA 91040
www.PendraigPublishing.com
Printed in the United States of America

ISBN: 978-1-936922-51-2

Dedication

I would like to dedicate this book to those who taught me the reality of magick:

To Dot and Reg Griffith,
aka Merlin and Morgana of the House of Avalon,
for nurturing my connection with the realms in my youth

To Nigel Bourne and Seldiy Bate,
for teaching me the basics so well

To Jackie, Angela, Pat, Aleph , Beth,
and the other coveners who worked with me in England

To Colin, my brother,
who encouraged my explorations

To Susan and Jay Mayer,
who introduced me to the love of my life

To Ann and Dave Finnin,
who introduced me to my Ancestors

To Raven and the coveners of Wildewood Grove,
who shared my journey into the Mysteries

To the coveners of Briar Rose,
who journey with me now

To all those who have enjoyed my books,
DVDs, podcasts and workshops,
who have given their love and their support
to my own personal brand of craziness!

To Jo-Ann, Tony and Michaela,
who have joined their creativity to mine.

To all of you, thank you — this book is as much yours as it is mine.

Acknowledgements

I would like to thank those who helped to bring this project to birth, namely the brave souls who participated in my Enchantment workshops:

Debbie Crossthwait	Anna Fofanna	Sharon Marlin
Sam Brown	Jeff Scrybe	Glenda Chism
Tamblyn	Oriana Miller	Solstice Henna
Annwyn Avalon	Tracy O'Neill	Jo-Ann Byers-Mierzwicki
Toni Nelson	Steve Silva	Melissa Charbs Willsy
Kevin Pappan	Ann Finnin	Sonja Barnes
Doug Helvie	Shae Medea	Emma Lambert
Susan Mayer	Jeff Neff	Simon Wood
Rion Kallady	Yvette Reece	Anna Strongwolf
Edward Friar	Dan Viera	Susan Chase
Linda Paddon	Renee Berg	Ellen Gee
Angela Rickman	Todd Norton	James Palmer
Tanya Newton	Michele Gilmer	Maurice Appling
Glenn Lane-Yule	Barbara Jones	Andrea Wills
Julie Forest	Amanda Armstrong	

...and thus share responsibility for what we are unleashing on the world:

Table of Contents

Photo Illustrations

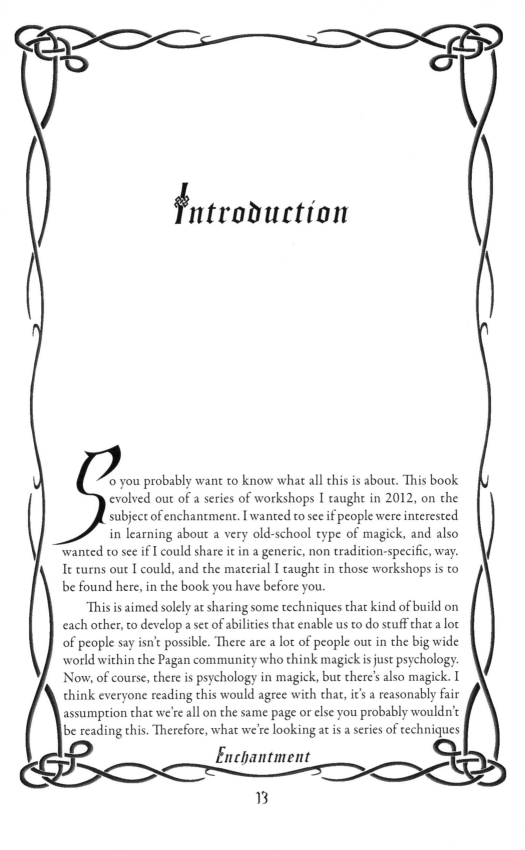

Introduction

So you probably want to know what all this is about. This book evolved out of a series of workshops I taught in 2012, on the subject of enchantment. I wanted to see if people were interested in learning about a very old-school type of magick, and also wanted to see if I could share it in a generic, non tradition-specific, way. It turns out I could, and the material I taught in those workshops is to be found here, in the book you have before you.

This is aimed solely at sharing some techniques that kind of build on each other, to develop a set of abilities that enable us to do stuff that a lot of people say isn't possible. There are a lot of people out in the big wide world within the Pagan community who think magick is just psychology. Now, of course, there is psychology in magick, but there's also magick. I think everyone reading this would agree with that, it's a reasonably fair assumption that we're all on the same page or else you probably wouldn't be reading this. Therefore, what we're looking at is a series of techniques and exercises that are designed to give us those classic witchcraft abilities and being able to — and I use the technical term here — to put the *fluence* on people: in other words, make them do our bidding.

I want to make it perfectly clear, though, that this isn't neural linguistic programming (NLP). A lot of stuff you find on line, that claims to tell you how to persuade people to do things they don't really want to do, is using NLP in a sales pitch, so people buy things they can't afford, don't want, and never liked in the first place. This isn't that. With the techniques you are going to work on in this book, you're going to be able to get those results without saying a word, from a distance — good old fashioned Jedi mind tricks. It really is possible to do stuff like this — I've done some of it in the past myself.

One thing is very important, though. It is the one thing that's kind of secret society; covenant-oriented about this thing... these exercises are cumulative. It isn't a case of being a kind of "technique of the week club", or even technique of the month club. The exercises you first learn, you're going to have to keep doing so the next exercises you learn have something to build upon. So they're all going to build on each other, and you're going to get more work to do. It really is worth doing. It's a bit like when you start going to the gym, you have to start easy, start light, do the simple stuff, and then as your stamina starts to build, you start doing longer and more difficult exercises. It is a matter of developing the mental and spiritual "muscles" to do the stuff you will learn later in this book.

How I Came upon Enchantment

Let's start off with a little bit of history — what caused this whole thing to happen in the first place? Well, I planned on writing a series of fiction books next. Last year, when I finally finished Visceral Magick, and I finally got that note from the printers saying it's up, it's for sale, I thought, great.

I had this whole trilogy of fantasy novels mapped out, ready to start writing it. The trouble was, as I read that email, into my head popped the next non-fiction book. So now after I've done this one, I'm going to try and get back to the fiction. One day I'll write my novels, but apparently I have at least this one to do first. It kind of landed fully fledged in my brain, complete with title and everything, and so I thought, ok, I'll do that, then. The seed that was planted, that grew into this book, actually goes right back to when I first started my formal training back in the early '80s in London, with the Alexandrian coven that I first trained with. Nigel and Seldiy who were HP and HPS of the coven, lived somewhere in south London, and so it was a horrendous train ride in the London underground, and then a bus to get to them, every Thursday night. Nine times out of ten I'd miss the last bus or the last train, and end up sleeping on the platform at Paddington. Which was not so bad — well, I was 18 at the time, so I didn't really care. It was fun, at least in the summer months when it wasn't piddling down with rain and blisteringly cold. After the coven had finished, there'd be just time to go down and get a round of beers in at the local pub. But this was a very, very popular pub, which meant when you walked in, there were about 20 people already at the bar trying to get their orders in, and you'd only have so much time left, because we'd only got there 20 minutes before last orders. So 20 people and 20 minutes meant that there was a fair chance we were not going to get our drinks.

So Nigel would set one of us a task of putting the '*fluence* on the barman so he would serve us first, and this was my introduction to enchantment, because you've got a guy who's busy dealing with other people, not even looking in your direction, and you have to get him to stop what he's doing, turn round, look at you, and take your order. Beer is a really great inspiration and incentive, especially on a hot summer's night, so we all developed reasonably good skills at getting the attention of the barman without having to resort to throwing somebody else's glass at him. That wouldn't have gotten us a drink anyway, so we didn't try that. We never got any formal training on this; it was a case of "we're being taught this great witchy skill for the purpose of getting beer".

In all fairness, Nigel and Seldiy trained under Alex and Maxine Sanders, and Maxine was notorious for learning how to unlock doors, because there was a locked door between her and the food that she wanted to eat when she was a starving student, and there was no door in London that could stay locked when she was around, by all accounts, when she was younger. So you see that basic instincts are a good incentive, which is what I'm trying to get at. So that's where this book from; over all the years — my years in Alexandrian Wicca,

Enchantment

and then coming over here and studying with the Roebuck, and then with Wildwood, and then Linda and I raising our own hearth here at Briar Rose — we've always focused on the deeper lore, and only really occasionally dipped back into remembering these very simple, very basic witchy skills that were there right at the beginning of my journey.

So now I think it is time that we take them out of the closet, dust them down and start putting them to good use again, because people forget they exist, and It seems like a good time, judging by the response of all my students out there around the world, to start looking at this material and saying don't forget it. So we're going to be doing some real magick — not that I'm saying you haven't done real magick before — but this is real magick of a sort that Hollywood would recognize as magick. Now, manipulative magick has been a big part of stories for millennia. It's where most of our knowledge of it comes from — the tales of witches and wizards and sorcerers and fairies, manipulating mere mortals into doing their bidding.

I mean, you can't open up a fairytale book without falling over a story of some wicked witch luring children to their doom in the forest, or enchanting some young maiden to fall in love with her ugly stepson, or whatever. There are all kinds of weird and wonderful stories, and that's part of the problem, because a lot of people say "it's a fairy story, it isn't true, it isn't real" — forgetting that most of those fairy stories are the folktales that contain the magical lore of our paths... of our ancestors... of our magical way of life, hidden in plain sight. So we can look at these tales and instead of thinking "oh, what a nice little fable", think "okay, what is the actual practical skill that turned into this story, and how can I get it?"

It's one of the many ways we can tap the bone — recover lost lore — by looking at the stories, the children's stories, the fairy tales, the folk tales, the legends and myths of our Gods and Goddesses, and cultural heroes. We need to look at what's happening in the stories — the stories of shape shifting, invisibility, flying, and making people do things against their will. And if you don't want to go back to Grimm's Fairy Tales, Celtic Wonder Tales and all the other story books, you know, maybe you just don't feel comfortable with children's stories anymore, or maybe you've never liked them in the first place...then go modern — Star Wars, with its Jedi mind tricks, is exactly what we're talking about.

Peter Paddon

Okay, we're not going to be throwing light sabers around this time, but we are going to learn some Jedi mind tricks. It's a real skill, and we're going to learn to do it. So I hope that makes some sort of sense.

The Ethics of Manipulation

Having said that, we do need to take a look at the ethics of manipulation. Now, some might say it is unethical to manipulate others, period. There's only one problem with that — every form of magick that exists is a manipulation of some sort. You're manipulating the Universe, the Earth, the elements, yourself, energy — you're manipulating something. So why not people? Well, there is a very strong ethical streak to this, and I want to make sure that we cover that along with the fun stuff because I would be unethical if I didn't.

I like to think that I'm ethical. We're all imperfect creatures, but you know, we can all strive to do the right thing, at least sometimes. Is it ethical to manipulate somebody into doing something against their will? We see this is the issue with ethics. An ethical code isn't like a moral code. A moral code is stuff like "Thou Shalt Not"... Thou shalt not kill, thou shalt not steal, thou shalt not covet thy neighbor's ass, a fairly familiar moral code; but the thing about moral codes is, you can follow them blindly — they're a set of rules. Do this, don't do that, and you'll be all right. But ethics aren't like that, because when you look at it from an ethical point of view, everything is relative, and black and white become a sliding scale: don't kill, except for when killing is the only thing you can do — when it's the thing you must do. Don't steal, except for when, if you don't steal, something worse is going to happen, like stealing food to feed a starving child, or stealing the secret weapon from the marauding warlord. Stealing third base — no, sorry, I'm getting a little carried away there. Actually that is ethical because it's part of the game. That's a totally different story. Ethics are all about shades of gray. It's about weighing up the consequences of your actions and deciding whether you are willing to pay the price, or to use the old fashioned term, "paying the coin". Don't do what you desire, do what is necessary is what Robert Cochrane is famous for saying, amongst those who actually know he existed. Don't do what you desire; do what is necessary. Do the thing that is needed, and sometimes the thing that is needed is to kill somebody. Somebody is trying to rape your child, you're not going to think twice about it, in most cases. Or at least, you're going to give it a good college try.

Sometimes you need to make someone do something that they don't want to do. Everyone who's a parent has had to do that on countless occasions: clean your room, pick up your toys...and that's just talking to your spouse. So it's very important to take an ethical approach to this, because there are times when you need to force, or need to be aggressive, or need to be violent or need to be strong, but you have to know that it's because it's necessary, not just because you're feeling pissed at somebody. There are times when we all want to choke the living shit out of somebody, but generally speaking it's ethically not a good idea.

The key is that we do what is necessary, and take responsibility for our actions — that includes accepting the consequences. It's all part of being a witch — I mean, there are a thousand different definitions of what a witch is, but for me, the only one that really matters is that a witch is somebody who takes responsibility for their actions and for their life, and they live it fully. That's part of what all this is about, because one of the things that happen when you start developing the skills that we're going to be exploring, you start to feel a lot more confident, which is really good because confidence is a very important part of the process. If you don't have confidence in yourself, it's going to be a major impediment to actually doing the practices, because you have to believe you can do it. That takes confidence, but it's also about living in the now.

Every time we go into ritual space, every time we work magick, we enter the now, we enter the realm between the worlds where time and space cease to exist, where all time is now, and all place is here. Where we can interact with every aspect of the universe, from its beginning to its end, however you define those — there's another discussion to be had — Ancestors long gone, ancestors yet to be. That's what we say every time we call the ancestors into our circle, because in non-linear time, where there is no time, what's to stop you meeting the ancestors that haven't been born yet. So we call them all in — we're not proud. The point is that, in order to work this stuff, you need to be able to get into that space easily and comfortably while still being functional in the mundane world.

Peter Paddon

18

And that's the rub, really. When you work like this, you're living in the now. When you look at most people, mundane people, everyday people, even us when we're being mundane, temporally, we're kind of a blur, because 90% of our concentration is on what happened 5 minutes ago and what might happen 10 minutes ahead. Very little of our consciousness is here and now. When you drive to work in the morning, how many of you are actually aware of the piece of road you're actually on? You're all thinking about what's round the next corner, or what's at the office when you get there.

How many of us even remember how we got to work in the mornings, most days? That is because we're not in the moment. We're in the future and in the past, you know, wishing we were back in bed and dreading what's going to be waiting for us when we walk in the office door. When you work magick, you have to be here and now. But luckily, while you're working magick here and now is everywhere and every when, so it kind of works for us. But it means that we come into focus where everyone else is a blur, we come into sharp relief and become very focused, and that's actually one of the best tools we have for manipulating the will of others. Because when you are focused and clear and present, people listen to you. Consciously or unconsciously they listen to you, and they see you as a figure of authority, and whatever you say they are inclined to do because most people are sheep. Even we are sheep, unless we're trying not to be. We're herd creatures, we're designed that way. We're wired that way.

That kind of brings us back full circle again, because when you have that much power over people, there's a temptation to overstep the boundaries a little. Ethics kicks in again, and we remember, do what is necessary — no more, no less. So some of the training exercises we're going to do that I'm going to give you to practice — remember, this isn't a once a month thing, it's an every-living-breathing-moment for the rest of your lives thing, if you really want to be serious about it — I'm going to give you some exercises to do, and they're kind of naughty. They're harmless "muscle-building" exercises, which makes it ethical, but they're naughty, because you're going to do things like, whilst waiting in line for your lunch, or for the check-out at the supermarket, or waiting for a bus, you're going to use these techniques to prod and poke and annoy the people around you, to build up those "muscles". So you're going to have fun. But you're going to be kind of brats. I hope you like that idea.

Enchantment

Magick, Stripped of Dogma and Rite

Now, what we are going to be focusing on for the entire book is magick, pure and simple. There's not going to be any dressing on this. I'm not going to go into cultural or religious or spiritual aspects of this at all. It's going to be pure technique, pure practice, pure theory and philosophy behind the practice. No tying it into the way the Celts did it, or the way the Romans did it or the way anyone else did it, because we're not all following the same path. All the people who are going to read this book aren't following the same path. So I'm just going to give the bare bones here, because the bare bones are the important part. You can then take those bare bones, and you clothe them in the tradition you follow, in the practice you follow.

You could add the incantation, the incense, the robes, and the sort of spiritual metaphysical explanations for it all later. Let's get the hard-cold techniques down first, and then we can add that other stuff. That way, we can all work without getting annoyed — "oh, we don't do it that way in our coven", because that gets really old really quickly, and it happens a lot in the Pagan community. Any time you have a class with a lot of people from different traditions coming together, the first thing that comes up is "oh, I wouldn't do that in our tradition". Great, go outside, and we'll call you back when we're done. There isn't going to be any of that in this book, because it's pure technique. Is everyone good with that? Good.

Why I Wrote This Book

Why did I decide to teach the series of workshops, and then write this book?. Well, it's fairly simple. I decided to do it because I got sick and tired of seeing person after person online, in chat rooms, in forums, at meet-ups, describing spells as prayer with props. Nothing invokes the urge to maim in me more than hearing someone saying that, a spell is just a prayer with props. Of course spells are not prayers with props. For starters, witches don't pray.

Prayer is an act of supplication and an act of worship. We do not worship our gods, generally speaking. That's an act of religion. Witches work with their deities, they work with their patrons, and they work with their ancestors. Any worshipping and supplicating and praying that is done, is done part of their religious practice, which is another thing entirely. Witchcraft is a magical practice that is usually expressed through a religious belief system, which is usually the one that you grew up in. In the 21st century, in this day and age in this part of the world, we have the luxury of being able to say "screw it: I don't like the religion I was brought up in, I'm choosing a different one and then I'm going to express my magick through that", and so we become Pagans. You can be Pagan without practicing magick. Look at 90% of Wicca these days. They actually turn their noses up at magick because they interpret "an it harm none, do as thou wilt" as saying magick is wrong, because of the "harm none" bit.

You can't do magick without causing harm to someone, is the argument. Of course, they forget that you can't breathe or eat without causing harm, either. Sorry, I'm not anti-Wicca, but I'm anti-that particular excuse. Believe me, I like magick — I want to do magick, and I don't just want to do psychology, I want to do real magick, and I've been doing real magick for a long time now. Nigel and Seldiy got me really on a good start, and it's been downhill ever since, really. That's the way it happens. This book has come out of a place of frustration for me, partly because nobody is teaching this stuff, and it is so fundamental and basic, because if you can do the manipulation stuff, if you can get into somebody's head and heart so much that they will believe whatever you put there, then you can take that and apply it to yourself and change yourself, and change the world around you. You may have gotten the idea that this is all about manipulating people, but it's not. It's about manipulating the world, the universe, and yourself. We're going to learn stuff to make us change as well. It's part of the process. The techniques that you're going to learn... it is kind of ironic, really, that in order to be able to put the manipulation on somebody else, the muscles that you have to build, the only way to build them is to work on yourself to start off with, because that's the equipment you have access to. Then you start working on your universe, because it's more malleable than a stubborn human, and then, when you've built up your muscles on that, then you can turn round and start working on people.

We always work on ourselves first, because change comes from within. But there's another very pragmatic reason, and this is going to

Enchantment

be a very pragmatic book. If you set about changing the universe to your liking, and then change yourself, the universe may not be to your liking anymore, and you'll have to change it again. If you change you first, you don't have to do so much work, and as I'm inherently lazy, it seems like a much more sensible way of doing things. So hopefully you'll all agree with that.

Peter Paddon

Prerequisites

So, what do you need to be able to do this stuff? Well, balls the size of medicine balls — no, just kidding. You do need to have some chutzpah. Which is a more polite way of saying the same thing, I guess. In an ideal world, you will be familiar with and practicing what I like to call visceral magick, and yes, that is a plug for my last book, *Visceral Magick,* available at all good bookstores.

Visceral Magick

You don't have to read the book to be able to do this stuff. It's just that it's a very simple and straightforward way of getting it if you don't already have it. If you follow a magical path, a spiritual path, that is about getting viscerally connected to the world and to your magick and to your gods, then you've already got what you need in that particular department. It's actually being invested in and connected

Enchantment

23

at the heart instead of at the head. As long as your magick is coming from the heart, then you're starting in the right place. If you're trying to do the ceremonial path — and I apologize to any ceremonialists who are reading this — ceremonial magick is the great intellectualization. There are exceptions, but the classic Golden Dawn magical system is very cerebral, and that kind of short-circuits the kind of magick that witches and shamans do.

Because it comes from the heart, and it defies logic; in fact, it often manifests in the form of paradoxes, and the two are mutually exclusive. If you try and intellectualize your magick whilst you're doing it, you will shut it down completely. Analyze it, dissect it, do what you like with it afterwards, but whilst you're working on it, you have to switch that off. A lot of ceremonial ritual, whether it's from ceremonial magick or from the formal ceremony in certain forms of witchcraft, has to do with giving your intellect something to do while the rest of you gets on with magick. It's kind of cosmic sleight of hand. That is just my opinion, but I'm very opinionated, so I'm forcefully stating it, and you're free to disagree with me, but that's the way it works from standing at the center of my particular universe. We all of course stand at the center of our own universes because we're living beings, and the universe we perceive subjectively puts us smack bang in the center of it.

Trance States

As magical practitioners, we are inherently placing ourselves at the center of the universe as we see it, because that is our rightful place as "master of the temple", even if the only temple we're master of is the one we're standing in, and even then we're only renting it. The practical key to everything we're doing is trance state. Magick and trance go together like brie and toast. Basically when we work magick we're in a trance state. How many of you do conscious trance work, trance exercises, whether it's meditation, astral projection, that sort of thing? Pretty much everyone who practices magick does this. This means that we have a head start, because for a lot of people, they don't get the whole trance state.

With ninety-nine percent of people joining a coven or taking a Wicca 101 class at the local metaphysical store, the thing you hear most often is "I really find it difficult to get into trance. It just doesn't come well for me", and then you sit and watch them trying to get into trance, and you watch them go purple with the effort. We've all seen it, and what do you think the problem is? They're trying too hard, and getting in their own way.

Now, pretty much everyone practicing magick is already doing trance work, so this is kind of remedial work for you, but I want to share it all, so it is in the book for the few who haven't tried trance work yet. Being in trance is something we do really easily. The trouble is, we usually don't know how to recognize it unless somebody points it out to us.

Now I know you are all going to know the answer to this anyway, but tough, it has to be said. How many people daydream? Pretty much everybody, and every time you daydream, you're going into a trance. The simplest definition of a trance is that it is an altered state of consciousness where your focus is beyond the real, the mundane, and we do it, on average, approximately every 10 minutes, give or take, because we're not very focused creatures as a species. We tend to drift off, unless our attention is being drawn by something like a good movie.

We tend to sort of drift off into the middle distance. A good example is just about any company meeting, especially if it's a town hall meeting. How many of you sat there, struggling to stay interested, until it's over. In your head, you're anywhere but in that room. That is trance. Trance is triggered really, really easily, and it's triggered by a lot of different things really easily. You could trigger it yourself just by focusing on it. That's all you have to do, turn your attention to it and there it is, and just don't try too hard. You can induce trance in other people — one of our students has been doing some path-workings, and she initially had some issues with getting into trance. I eventually taught her my little secret trick — that I tell everybody — about using oils, which I'll share later.

But the first time we really got good results, I did a purely physical thing: I lifted her skull off of her vertebrae just a fraction of an inch, for a couple of seconds. That's all it took — you take the pressure, the weight of the skull, off of the neck, just ever so slightly, that's all it takes to put someone in a trance. We will be examining this technique a little further on in the book. Of course, the trick is, if you do it, and they get

Enchantment

in deep enough, their neck will be limp, and their head will fall if it isn't supported, and that's what happened to our student the first time we did it with her.

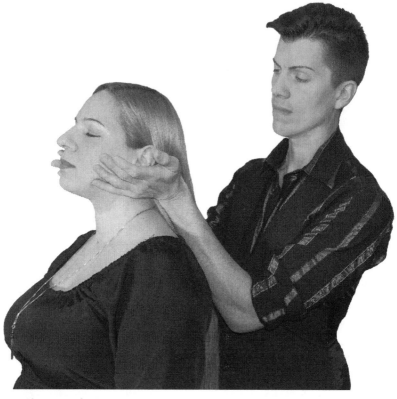

She went deep into trance straight away, but she was in a chair with no head support, and I didn't want to let go. I had to wait until she came out again. Now in classical witchcraft, this is known as opening the gate to the ancestors.

Because what it does it, it opens up a space at the base of the skull, at the back, which is the traditional gateway that spirits and ghosts enter in during possession. We are preconditioned — it's a bit like if you turn a chicken upside down, it goes limp, exactly the same mechanism. You go into trance, and so does the chicken. We, however, do not lay eggs, and hopefully your next step after putting somebody into trance isn't going to be to wring their neck, because that would not be a good thing.

Peter Paddon

There are other very simple trance techniques. Now, the one I was talking about earlier that many of my students love using and sharing with people, is a little trick I picked up. I used to be an aromatherapist. I trained under my brother who's a very, very accomplished holistic therapist. He has a doctorate in naturopathy, and also doctorate of acupuncture and a whole lot of qualifications. He's certified as a medical doctor by the Geneva World Health Organization, in Geneva, and he's one of Canada's foremost teachers of holistic therapies. But before he did all that, he was a teacher of aromatherapy back in England, and he taught me aromatherapy. Now, this is something I came up with myself, but based on what he taught me. One of the things about the human brain is that it's divided into two halves. The left brain, apart from taking care of the right-hand side of the body, is the logic circuitry. It's the analytical, intellectual area. Some of us find it works better than others.

The right brain on the other hand, is Mister Creative, Mister Actor, Mister Thespian, Mister Artist, Mister Drawing Maniac if given the right circumstances — and that's part of the problem because magick really works a lot on the right side of the brain, but we need to understand it with the left side of the brain. The left side of the brain hits the off switch whenever it encounters it, and that's why we have to have suppression. In western society we tend to live a lot in our left brain. We tend to be, despite appearances in some cases, very logical, scientific and intellectual, and that gets in the way. So I thought to myself, there's got to be some way I can use all these wonderful oils to get round that problem.

It happened that I was reading at the time about some experiments that were done back in the '50s, where psychologists had noticed that there are people who, for one reason or another, have the bridge between the two hemispheres of the brain severed in an accident, or it doesn't form right in their development. So essentially, their two brains aren't connected, the left brain and right brain are totally separate. They noticed that people who have this particular issue, have experiences like they know what a thing is, they recognize it, but they can't tell you what it's called, because the memory of it, the knowing of what it does, and what you can do with it, was quite happily in the creative right brain, but the name for it was in the left brain, and the two weren't speaking to each other.

Enchantment

So, they thought, well, let's do some experiments, actually prove some theories here — and I can't remember what they were trying to prove, but they basically operated on a lot of people and severed that bridge, which was not a very good idea, because people who have that bridge severed aren't particularly functional in a modern day society. But it backed up their theories, and somewhere along the way they realized they could actually do it temporarily with chemicals. So they'd give people drugs that temporarily separated their brain hemispheres. I thought, well, I don't have access to pharmaceuticals, but I thought, I do have access to all these wonderful oils. So I started having a look at the properties of oils, and I finally came up with this, and it's very, very simple and very elegant. Just need two oils — frankincense and clary sage.

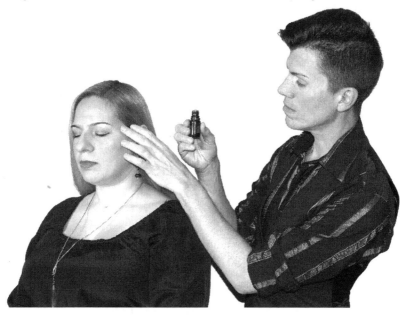

If you have any difficulty getting into trance state, this will sort you out. Now, frankincense is known as a meditative — that's why they use it in religious ceremonies throughout the world, is because it automatically puts you into a meditative state. It puts you into a prayerful state. It mellows you out, not in that stoner sense, but it puts you into a contemplative state. So it makes great church incense, and it is used to calm people down. Clary sage, on the other hand, is used most in aromatherapy for dealing with drug addicts, when they're trying to get clean. You replace the buzz of the drug with the buzz of the oil, because it's known as a euphoric — it promotes euphoria. It smells like a wet tea bag, so I haven't quite figured out the correlation, but it works — I tried it out, and it worked. If you take frankincense oil and put a dab of it on your pulse point on your right wrist, and on the pulse point behind your right ear, and on your right temple, and under your right nostril; and you take clary sage and you do exactly the same points on the left-hand side of your body, the frankincense takes your intellect to church, and it kneels down in the pew and starts praying and being all contemplative. Meanwhile, the creative side, the right brain, wakes up and says hi, and you get this dichotomy between the two halves of the brain that takes you straight out of mundane reality and places you between the worlds. I don't recommend doing it too much because you'll get dependent on it, not in the sense of like "I need my frankincense", but more in the sense of I can't do it without it anymore. Use it as a stepping stone, not as a crutch is what I'm saying.

Focus and Will

So that is the brief discussion about trance states. The other things you need are focus and will. We all have ADD moments, we all have problems focusing from time to time, but when it comes to magick, one of the most important things we can do is focus. That is one of the reasons why that altered state is necessary, apart from the fact that it gives you access to the realms and all the metaphysical stuff for whatever path you're following. The very simple, practical thing being in a trance state does is it places you in a place with no distractions, because if you're in the now, you're not going to notice the television in the next room.

It isn't easy to get totally focused on what you're doing, and that's what you need to do for any magical work — you have to be totally focused on the work, and even in trance state that takes a bit of skill. Especially if you go into a deep enough trance that you're seeing little sparkly things, because then you get distractions again, but this time they're in there with you. But learning to focus is one of the reasons, another reason why we have ritual structure. So when we're working as a group, the ritual serves to get us all focused on the same thing at the same time. It keeps us all on the same page of the script, if you like. When we're working on our own, we don't necessarily need follow a structured ritual format.

But there isn't a magical equivalent of putting all the ingredients in the bowl, mixing them, pouring them in the pan, putting it in the oven, and then going away and waiting for 20 minutes, because, if you're working magically, you don't have an equivalent of a gas oven — you are the gas oven. So you're tromping around the circle pushing energy into what you're doing, until it's done. It keeps you focused. The other thing that goes hand-in-hand with focus is will, and will is a very slimy character, because it's one of those things that you have to define. There are an awful lot of people in the Pagan community who are familiar with two different rules that get bandied about a lot: "And it harm none, do as thou wilt" and "do as thou wilt is the whole of the law". There's way too many people who read the word "will" in those and think it means "I can do what I like". No it doesn't, because as we said at the beginning, "do not do what you desire; do what is necessary" — that is what will is about, doing what is necessary. Doing what it is your will to do. It's an awkward sentence structure, but I hope you're getting the point. There's an old traditional saying that to work magick, there has to be a need, and this is a quaint way of saying the same thing. Now, when we hear need, I've heard people give the argument that it means you can't do stuff you just want, there has to be a need, like for world peace, or to feed the hungry, or to heal somebody. You can't do it to get a dozen beers, or a dozen doughnuts or whatever. Well, yes you can, you just have to really need beer, or really need the doughnuts, because what you have to do is, you have to be passionate about what you're doing. If you don't feel any passion, you're not going to get any results, and the passion helps you focus as well. So when we talk about will, we're talking about doing whatever it is that you have to do, but we're also talking about being invested in it. Not just doing it because it seems like a good idea, but because you really need to do it. You're passionate about it, and you feel strongly about it. Magick is driven by emotions, powerful emotions provide the energy for magick, whether it's anger, joy, laughter, sex, lust — they all work indiscriminately.

There could be a positive or a negative emotion, but it needs strong, powerful emotions to drive magick. That means you need to be passionate, that means it needs to be your will that this be done so. In ancient Egypt, the adepts were known as Maa-Kheru, which literally means "truth-speaking". This doesn't mean that they always told the truth. In fact, to be honest, they were lying duplicitous bastards half the time because they were politicians as well as magicians. What it meant is the words they said became true. This is the definition of magick. What you will becomes true, and that's what this book is really all about. I know I should point out, that when we get to the end of this book; it's not going to end there. I'm not quite sure where it goes next, but I'm sure there are another two books in this somewhere — that once we've all got this under our belt, there's another step to take, involving more manifestation magick, and then beyond that, doing stuff that's totally ridiculous, but so ridiculous I can't figure out what it is yet. We have to take step two before we'll know what step three is, I guess, but I know that there's a step from this book on enchantment, the next one will be a manifestation book.

Visualization

The other skill we need is visualization. You need to be able to see things. Now, and we're not talking daydreaming here, although that's the start of it. Being able to visualize things clearly and strongly is an important part of magick. You can work magick without it, but it's so much harder, because there's a secret, and it's one, I give away almost every class I teach.

This doesn't always make it into people's books, but it's real, nevertheless. The real secret to magick, to working a spell, is whatever the outcome of the spell is, you have to be able to see it so clearly at the fulcrum point of the spell, of the crafting; you have to see it so clearly that, just for a second, you believe it's already come true. You get that happening in your crafting, and then you've done it. You don't need to do anything else. You will guarantee success. So the stronger and clearer you can visualize, the more likely you are to get that, just a fraction of a second, where you believe it's already happened, but once you've done that, it is certain to come to pass. Of course, it takes years of training and skill to get yourself to that point.

A very dear friend of mine commented that children get this concept of believing the thing has already happened much easier, because they

Enchantment

are not bogged down with mundane things the way adults are, plus they still believe that every fantasy is already real. She told me about when she bought her daughter a Spell-Casting Barbie. Her daughter was four years old at the time, and she told the girl to make a wish and believe as they stirred the ingredients that came with the doll. Six months later, as they were flying to Australia, her daughter asked if she remembered helping her cast the spell with her witch Barbie, and my friend said yes... it turns out that her daughter had put her belief into her mother and herself going on a trip far away together. I'm pleased to say that both she and her daughter, quite a few years later, are still crafting their magick and creativity, though I think Barbie may have retired from the team.

If you've already been on this path a long time, consciously or unconsciously, I'm hoping that this means that you can get to that point. Now there are two important things to add. Number one is that this isn't a race, ok? People develop at different rates. Some of you will take to this like a duck to water. You'll be quacking and paddling all over the place, "oh, this is great, this is easy, oh, look at me", juggling stars and dancing on the moon, but some of the others will be sitting there going "hey, what about me?" Well, those that take a more scenic path frequently turn out to be the people at the end who are better at it, because sometimes it takes a little while for the practice to come to fruition within you. Sometimes you have to bring the water to the boil before things start happening.

It might take longer to get there, but once you get there, boom — really spectacular results, and people are going to have different levels of ability. I think everybody who is reading this is going to get to a level of competency. We're all going to be able to do this stuff by the end. Some people will be able to do it better, more flamboyantly, more excitingly, than others, because for them, this is going to be their niche. Other people may have their niche somewhere else, and they'll be OK at this, but it's not the best thing they do, and that's fine. We're all different. If we were all the same, it'd be really, really boring, and we wouldn't sell any books. We'd already know how to do it all. The fact that we're all different is something we should celebrate, and when you have somebody who is better at visualization than other people, or somebody who is better at putting in energy than others, you know what you do? You team up.

Peter Paddon

There's always going to be Jack of all trades who can do a bit of everything, and there's going to be specialists. If you find you're a specialist, and there is a part of this you are better at than others, then you might find it useful to team up with a person, or a couple of people, who fill the gaps, and you work together. Between you, you make a kick-ass team and get results. That's why traditionally witches were found in 3's or 5's or 9's — it always seems to be an odd number. On the magical path, we're all individual people, but this doesn't have to be a solo exercise. You can team up and do things together. You can build a magical circuit with people; someone who's a good energy-raiser, someone who's a good visualizer, somebody who's good at drawing everything into a single point of focus, and all of a sudden you've got a ritual crew that can kick butt like nobody's business. Does that make sense? Cool.

Confidence

I mentioned confidence at the beginning. Now, it may surprise you to know that I'm a fairly shy person. If you really look at me, I'm shy. You'd never know that when you watch me teach a workshop, because my "teaching persona" is all an act. I could not do it as me. I'm putting on a persona to do it, and it's simply a role I play. I'm actually a very private, shy person who doesn't like standing out in a crowd, believe it or not, but it's all about confidence. The reason why I put on a persona is that when I'm wearing a persona, I have all the confidence in the world. I'm actually certain that what I'm doing is right and true and perfect. It's before and after I get all the doubts. When I used to do a lot of stage acting, I used to get stage fright after I came off stage, which is a much more practical way of doing it.

But while I was on stage, I was the actor; and when I'm in front of a class, I'm the teacher; and when I'm in front of the altar, I'm the priest. They are roles I play, and why, when I put on those hats, well, I put on the confidence that goes with them. So you don't have to be a big, beefy strapping tally-ho, Brian Blessed of the Pagan world, in order to get results from this, but you have to be able to put on your Brian Blessed tee shirt occasionally, and let your inner Brian Blessed out for some exercise. Does everyone know who Brian Blessed is? Well, if you've seen Kenneth Brannagh's Henry V, he's the big dude with a beard. The only guy wearing real armor and chain mail, because it was his own. He has a big, big booming voice.

Enchantment

I'm sure you get the idea even if you don't know who he is. Confidence is something that you can fake to a certain extent, because if you behave confident, you kind of start feeling confident. A bit like if you're feeling sad, smile, because it's very difficult to stay sad whilst you're smiling. Laughter really is the best medicine, because it pulls you out of the sadness of feeling crappy. By going through the motions you can sometimes actually kick start the real thing, and so we put on our confident persona, we put on our magical self. That's why so many secret societies have these secret teachings about assuming the magical persona or the "body of light". When you put on your robe, and your ring of power, and your lamen of authority, and everyone refers to you as Frater So-and-So of the lodge — this is putting on Mister Confident.

Peter Paddon

On a more prosaic level, people do this when they go out, well, as we quaintly call it in England, going out on the pull. When you get your best cologne and douse yourself liberally with it, put on your least unclean shirt, perhaps open to the waist with a medallion, and you go down to the pub. Inside you're quivering with fear, but all they see is the "hey, baby" persona. You're putting on an act; you're putting on a persona to hide your own fears, and what happens is that it's infectious; you get drawn into it, and you begin to live the role. Of course, with some of these roles, it's really handy to be able to put them back in the closet afterwards. You don't want to go into the office on a Monday morning and announce, "Hi, I'm Frater the Magnificent!"

Mind you, I do know people at work, who perhaps need to put their weekend persona away safely when they come to work, but I work in the entertainment industry, so what do you expect? Confidence is very important. If you second-guess yourself, you're never going to get to that point where you are absolutely certain it's already happened.

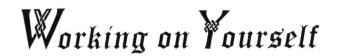

Working on Yourself

*L*ater on, you're going to want to use a small crystal. Ideally, a quartz crystal pebble is the thing to start with. This is the kind of thing you want. It doesn't have to be perfectly round. Just has to have no edges or facets or points on it — it has to be a pebble, in other words. It doesn't have to be perfect inside — my one has some rutilation in there, but it doesn't matter. Get one that feels right... rummage around in the basket or whatever there is in the store and find one that feels right, and while you're there, pick up a black velvet bag. It doesn't matter what style it is, as long as it closes up and you can keep your rock in it when you're not using it, and that you can lay it in the palm of your hand and use it as a backdrop for the crystal when you're using it.

That's why I specified black velvet. You can actually keep it in any old thing, but you need something black and matte, to rest it on while you're working with it, when we get to that exercise later in this book.

Enchantment

Trance Techniques

As I said before, getting into trance is actually a lot easier than most people think; it's actually knowing what the target is as much as anything else. The simplest way of getting into trance is really very simple indeed. If you stand on your feet, shoulder width apart — this isn't essential, it just gives you a level of stability and it's conducive to the exercise. When you get to be able to do this naturally, you don't need to do the technique, you just go into it, but for now there's some physiological stuff you can do that will help you get in a little easier. When you're standing with your feet shoulder width apart, it's a little easier to just flex your knees a little, drop your center of gravity down a bit.

What you want to do is to gently bob — I don't want you to bounce, because that will get really aerobic. Just let the springiness of your knees, those of you that have knees that spring, just let yourself bob gently, it doesn't have to be fast, either, just gentle bob, like you're sort of floating in the ocean, just getting billowed by the waves, and already you can

Peter Paddon

feel it coming in. Feel that? If you add to that, drop your shoulders, let your spine curve a little, and if you bring your shoulders forward, as if you were pretending to hold a beach ball, then get your shoulders in roughly the right position, then you can let your hands drop down, but keep your shoulders more or less where they were.

So you've got curved shoulders, curved spine. Your center of gravity is lowered, and you're kind of floating in the ocean of life. You can really feel how relaxed that feels, and if you let yourself down slowly and gently sway from side to side, you really start to feel like the eddies and currents of the universe are shifting you. It's almost like minimalist tai chi, and that's all it takes. If you have gammy knees, don't do it too long, obviously. You can straighten your knees, and let your hips sort of sway from side to side, but from the hips, so you are kind of sashaying in place a little bit. If you have gammy hips, then just let your shoulders go backwards and forwards, so that somewhere there is movement beyond just the swaying. It turns the sway into some sort of undulation. Some part of your body is performing a figure of 8, which just accelerates the process, and that is really all it takes to get into a nice gentle trance that will let you focus on the work you're doing. So you can relax. If you're working with a partner, you can carefully do the head lifting.

This is two things in one, because this is a technique if you're working with a partner, the way you can help your partner to get into trance really easy. It's also one of the first manipulation techniques, because it's a way of gaining control of someone, making them suggestible. So when you're working with a partner, you're helping them get into trance. When you're manipulating somebody, you're also putting them in a trance state where they're suggestible, and it's probably, I'm afraid to say, most popularly been used as a seduction technique. It's really very simple, and it comes straight out of the teachings of Anton Mesmer. It involves gentle stroking in a downward direction, any part of the body. You'll feel the effect it is having on you very quickly; really, this is all it takes, so you do that a couple of times, and take their hands.

When you do that, they kind of automatically try to push down on it, and that accelerates the process. So it really is that simple to get somebody in a trance, and that one will work on someone who doesn't plan on getting into a trance. You can take someone by surprise with this. So that's one to really exercise your ethics. You could be standing

Enchantment

behind someone in a queue — that's an English word for a line — and if you can get enough focus into it before they turn around and slap you in the face you can totally take control of their mind.

There's a version of this which works really well with babies. If you're ever babysitting a screaming baby, from the bridge of the nose up, just gently stroke, it'll put them right to sleep. It's difficult to manipulate a baby because they don't have the language skills, but you could at least get them to rest for a bit, and it's not cruel. That is a totally ethical use of it. There are other ways you can get into trance — by yourself. You can't lift your own skull very easily, but what you can do is use some of the postures that the ancient Egyptians used. The god form postures are very good for getting into trance state.

The Egyptians were very fond of straight backs, whether they were sitting or standing, and they always show the knees at right angles when seated. The statues were very symbolic and they were symbolic because they were conveying technique, and so they were very rigid and formal for that reason. But some of the things we can learn, from the postures that the ancient Egyptians shared with us, are techniques that take you between the worlds, take you to meet the gods. Some of them are very overt, like the sign of Osiris risen, which is used in the Golden Dawn, which is also the mummy position. Energetically, it does things to your aura.

Enchantment

The only way I can really describe it, it's like your "wings" get folded in, and so it brings you to a sedate state of being, very calm and centered. When you want to project energy, the Egyptians would always have the left foot forward, because that gives you a foundation to push energy out. When you see gods seated, they're always sitting with their hands on their laps, and it's difficult to see without knowing a lot about anatomy and knowing a lot about art and ancient Egyptian art in particular, but there's a particular way they sat with their heads in a particular position. This is where you basically you take your own skull, and you can do this sitting in any position, you don't have to sit like an Egyptian for this. You kind of let your head go down, and then your chin goes forward and up. You're kind of elongating your neck slightly.

You could do it the other way by leaning forward and up as well, but it kind of works better if you actually elongate the neck back, and then tilt your head up ever so slightly. It does that same opening of the gate of the ancestors at the back. It doesn't give you the taking the weight off aspect of somebody else lifting your skull, but it does all the other parts, and it will actually work better when you're sitting or standing, but it opens up the "satellite dish", the crown chakra or the golden bowl, the Cauldron of Wisdom for the Celts amongst us. It opens it up to connect with the other realms. It is so simple to do, very, very easy.

So let's take a closer look at trance techniques. Now, you remember earlier I mentioned how just lifting somebody's skull, taking the weight of somebody's skull from their neck very quickly and very simply puts you into a nice, light trance. Well, I'm going to show you how to do it by yourself. Another technique that essentially does the same thing that you can do by yourself without having to have someone else get their hands round your throat. If you have somebody to work with, start by doing the skull-lifting technique, so you can compare the effect of the two techniques. Find the jaw line, and just rest the jaw line against your fingers, so that the back of the palm, the heel of your palm is kind of resting under the ears, and you literally just lift ever so slightly just enough to take the weight a bit, about a quarter of an inch, tops. You're not trying to wrench their heads off, just a quarter of an inch, just enough to take the weight — it is ever so simple —and then gently settle the skull back down again once you let them feel it for a few seconds, and switch round, so the other person can try it. We do go into trance remarkably easy. It's a little-known fact, and it's one that stage hypnotists make unfair use of on a daily basis, that it is really easy to put a person into trance, because we're doing it all the time. Every time you daydream, every time you wander away for a moment, you're in trance. It's as simple as that. Antoine Mesmer, with his animal magnetism, used this as a basis of his mesmeric techniques, and he got very, very complicated with it because he felt people needed a shove — you really don't — and he found out once he got discredited, he realized you don't need to shove, and he continued working quietly without the fancy gizmos and the bathtubs and iron copper rods and all the rest of it. He got rid of them because he realized you didn't need them anymore, and there are people today who still practice the mesmeric technique. Some of them do it for stage conjuring, some of them do it for therapy, and some of them do it for the power.

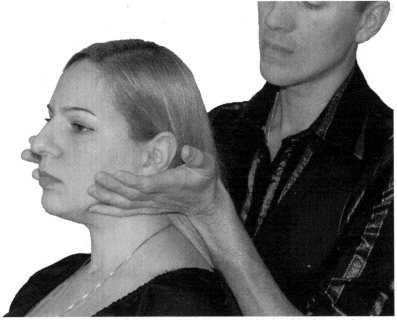

Now remember, what we're aiming at with this book is to learn to enchant by various techniques, in a purely magical way. We're not doing neuro-linguistic programming, we're not doing psychology; we're doing magick, but it's very simple and raw and basic and, hopefully, fun.

Enchantment

Another very simple technique that we use to get into trance very quickly — and if any of you have been in circle with me, you'll have seen me do this, because all of our guys do this — rocking. Back in the days of Raven's Flight and Wildewood coven, we used to call it the Wildewood shuffle, because we'd all do it. In Briar Rose Coven we all do it now, and it's actually a very minimalistic version of Seidhe. Seidhe (pronounced "seeth-eh") is a Germanic technique, the Seidhe tradition for want of a better word. It's part of the Germanic-Norse culture. It's what Odin was good at, and he was ridiculed by the other gods, despite being the boss god, because Seidhe was seen as a woman's technique. But that's only because the women kept it to themselves because it was bloody good. A full seidhe, well, if you come to my workshop on invocation at any time you will see, once again, a very basic seidhe, because it's one of the possession techniques I demonstrate. It's a kind of involuntary rocking, spasm, twitching thing, and it's kind of scary if you don't know what's going on, but it's fun to do. In many cases, though, just rocking from side to side is enough, it sort of does the same thing as lifting the skull. It takes you away a little bit, and I'll get you to try that in a minute, after the technique I'm going to show you now, because I'm now going to show you how to do the skull lifting by yourself. It's actually my interpretation of an old Celtic technique. I know it as opening the ancestral gates, because traditionally when the ancestors and the gods come in for a possession, or just to have a chat, they traditionally come in through the back of the base of the skull, and this technique is designed to provide easy access, open the gates, which are known as the ancestral gates, or gates of the ancestors.

It is a very simple technique — you start off just getting yourself in a comfortable position. I find for any sort of work like this, having your feet slightly wider than normal, sort of shoulder width apart, a bit like martial arts, gives you a little bit more stability, and allows for that side to side shuffle without any effort, and this is all coming from the hips, by the way, when you do that. You're not moving your whole body, you're just sliding your hips. It's like a very slow cha-cha-cha. So you start off, get yourself in a comfortable wide stance. Trance work, like much in martial arts, often works better if you drop your center of gravity slightly, and the easiest way to do that is just to flex your knees a little. That also lets your sideways motion be a lot smoother. It kind of lubricates the joints a bit. Of course, if you have gammy knees, you're not going to be able to do this for long, in which case just stand there, it's fine, and this is totally a posture thing, and it's a little bit involved because you have to sort of go through a couple of movements to get into the right posture. Start off by dropping your head down, sort of almost chin on your chest, type, so your neck is now curved. Then move your chin forward, and then bring it up so you're actually looking up slightly. What that does is it by doing that it's almost like a swan dive with just your head, standing in place. What it does is it leaves you with your head, your skull, tilted up slightly with your neck fully extended, so there is a gap between the vertebrae in your neck, and that physically makes the gap at the base of the skull more accessible. But more importantly, it essentially frees up the kinks, and lets you be alert but relaxed, which is what you need for trance state. Trance state, for anyone who isn't sure, is not to do with being "out of it", although that comes easy enough.

Basically the movement will get you there, the swaying will keep you there, but allow you to remain alert, because you don't have to focus on staying at the same consciousness level, because it kind of goes on auto-pilot as you rock from side to side. That's not going to make

Enchantment

you go deeper, but it's going to stop you coming back out, so you can prolong the process with the swaying, which can be very useful. Now, why do we want to get in trance? The answer is because it allows us to connect with the energy better. Visualization and energy manipulation is easier to do when you're in that "now space". When we do ritual or craft, whatever tradition we do, we go into a light trance to do the work because in order to be doing magick, you need to be in the now, the "no time, no space, all time is now, all space is here" place. That's when you can move the universe, because it's all here, now, and when past, present and future are all now, you can set things in motion that had to start 10, 15 years ago, 100 years ago, a thousand years ago, to bring about the changes that you need now, because you're in touch with all of it. Time isn't linear, nor is space; we just perceive it that way, and going into this altered state of consciousness enables us to put away that false perception. So once we get into that trance state, we then have to focus and we have to visualize. There's very little magick that goes on without some sort of focus and visualization, and even then, there is still focus and visualization at a subconscious level; it's just provided externally. When you have a powerful visceral experience, it grabs you and drags you instead of you having to aim, shoot and fire yourself, as it were. So focus and visualization are important.

Focus and Visualization Techniques

The thing about focus and magick is that it doesn't necessarily mean the same thing as focus in the mundane world, because if I asked you to focus on a box on the table, if you want to focus really hard, you would stare intently at the box, but, if you want to focus on it magically, you're more likely to gaze past it, and look a lot less focused, because we're not trying to focus our physical sight on the subject, we're trying to focus our mental sight, our magical sight, our spirit vision on them. That's a little tricky to do, because our physical vision gets in the way to a certain extent.

Anyone who does any form of scrying has got a head start here, and also, anyone who is really good at those 3-D images, because the trick in both cases is to look at it out of focus. So you focus on the thing by looking at it out of focus. Now, some of you may have taken my class on developing the sight, either in person or via the DVD I released some years ago, and when I teach the technique to see auras, it's a prime example of just exactly how this works. So here is that little technique, for those who haven't tried it before. It never hurts to repeat exercises, you can't repeat this too many times. So I want you to look at someone who is standing across the room, gaze at them. If you do not have someone to practice on, you can use your own reflection in a mirror. What I want you to do is look over their right shoulder, and you could interpret that however you like – their right shoulder, or the shoulder on the right from where you're standing, it doesn't matter. I want you to look at over their shoulder, and pick a spot on the wall behind them.

Then I want you to focus your physical sight on that spot, whatever it is, and the first thing you'll notice is the person goes slightly out of focus, because you're not focused on them. That's cool because what you're doing now is you are bringing your peripheral vision in to bear on the person, and there's a very interesting thing about human eyesight, and that is the fact that the center of our field of vision

Enchantment

has predominately cones which are the cells that detect color. But around the periphery of our vision are the rods, which don't pick up color because they're monochrome, but they're really good at picking up movement, and the thing is that when you're looking with your peripheral vision as something, you'll detect anything moving, such as energy. What happen is after a minute or so, you start to see a sort of wispy smoky something around them.

At this point, it's really tempting to focus on them to see what it is — don't, because if you do, you'll have to start again. If you can stare at it for a little longer, you'll start to notice that it's actually a layer of mist, and that's part of the aura, that's the etheric layer, which is the electromagnetic field around the human body. It's the easiest part of the aura to see, and it is basic life force. If you keep practicing this every day, you'll eventually be able to see the whole aura in glorious Technicolor. The reason this works is because we can all already see the aura energy, we're just used to filtering it out. What you're doing is tricking your mind, because your mind is already getting all this information from your subtle senses. It's just we've been conditioned through our childhood and adulthood to ignore this stuff, and your brain is actually really good at filtering out stuff that it's ignoring.

So you learned how to not see energy, and now you have to retrain yourself to see it, and this is a really good exercise for developing the right kind of focus, because you get instant obvious results. The more of the aura you can see, the better you're getting at focusing, and you don't need to have another warm body to practice on, although it's more fun that way. You can also practice on your hand — and before the rude comments start, let me explain. When I was a teenager, like many teenagers, I had nights where I couldn't sleep. I was at boarding school, so it's not like I could get up and traipse into the kitchen and gorge myself silly on leftovers from the fridge. Boarding schools don't let you do that. So I'd be lying there unable to sleep in this pitch black room with 18 other guys snoring or farting in their sleep.

Short of finding things to throw at them to start a fight, I was left to my own devices. Couldn't get to sleep, couldn't go anywhere, so I had to do something. So I'd stick my hand up in the air in the darkness, and practice seeing my own aura. I actually got to a point where I could see the energy so clearly it obscured my physical hand. This is something

I want you to practice; this is homework, ok, ladies and gentlemen. When you're lying in the dark before you go to sleep at night, when you're lying there in bed in the dark, or if you wake up in the night, you remember to try this. Or if you just shut yourself in a closet or something at work. You look at your aura around your hand, and keep going 'til you see the colors vividly.

What the colors are doesn't matter at this point — this particular book isn't about diagnosis through seeing the aura or anything like that. I don't care what the colors are. We're not going to talk about what they mean, because it's not relevant to manipulation (there are plenty of books available about auras and the magical meaning of colors). This is a means to an end, because once you can see the colors really strongly, you'll get to the point when you can see the colored light so clearly that it obscures the physical hand. That's the point I want you to try and get to. You should be able to do it if you do it every night, you should be able to reach that goal in 2 or 3 weeks. Some people may take a little longer, some people might get it straight away. When you get to the point where you can obscure your hand with the light of your aura, you can start visualizing energy coming from your heart center down your arm, so you're basically boosting the energy in your hand.

If you then visualize the energy that you're pushing through as a kind of deep amethyst purple, this is one of the classic techniques for invisibility, and the trick is, in the middle of the night with your hand stuck up in the air, what you're eventually aiming for when you get to that point is to try to make your hand disappear. When you can do it in the dark of night, start working on doing it in daylight, and if you really want to freak people out, once you've got good at doing it to your hand, do it to your face when you're talking to someone. I freaked my nephew out many years ago, because he was insisting on telling me deep and meaningful secrets of his life and I was bored as hell because what he thought were deep meaningful secrets, everybody knew. Plus he was just a punk, and a trouble maker, and I just wanted him to change the subject. I was bored, and so rather than just saying shut up, I thought, well, you know, I'm sitting here on a gate, by a field, in the countryside, not doing anything. You know what? I'm going to practice this technique I've been working on: and I made my face disappear, and he practically crapped himself.

It was fun, but then I'm evil that way. That's dodgy ethics, but he deserved it really. It turned out when we'd had a break-in and had some electronic stuff stolen, it was one of his friends, and he'd let them in, and so I'm not that upset about treating him cruelly. So play with your auras. Use it as a tool to help you develop your magical focus, and then use it to scare someone. Then you get objective evidence that something is working, and one of the things that you're going to find with this whole process is it's the objective results you get form other people that's going to build up your self-confidence.

So please, mess with people. The other thing is once you develop the ability to see energy flow, that's the point where I want you to start to visualize tapping people on the shoulder in the line in front of you. See if you can get them to turn round, because that's fun, too. Incidentally it's also handy if you want to learn to use a crystal ball, but we're not teaching that in this book, either.

Visualization is something we all need to be able to do. Now, if you aren't sure of what visualization is, it's having, and holding, an image in your mind or in your heart, but it's easiest to think of it as being in your mind, although the way you really want it to be, in the end, is in your heart. It is picturing things, and once again, there's a misconception; a lot of people think to do magick you have to have this sort of glorious Technicolor-"Spielbergian" special effects by Industrial Light and

Magic — affair going on, where if anyone else walked past, oh, my god, because they can see it too. This is not true at all. If you buy a lottery ticket and for a moment picture what you'd do with the money if you won, that is visualizing. The trick is, you have to do the things that go with the visualization to make it happen, and that's part of what this is all about. Because although this book is about manipulating other people, the techniques we are learning also can be used to manipulate ourselves and the universe. Just manipulating the person on the other side of the room, or the person behind the counter at the DMV, or the bartender at the bar, is a terrible waste. I mean it's good practice, don't get me wrong, but there's so much more you can do with it. In fact, this whole thing is going to be kind of backwards because the techniques I'm going to teach you first are the most important ones, in the whole book, because these are the ones that will change the universe for you, but the trick is, you start doing them now, because they help you develop the skills to do the manipulation of other people in different ways, and as you practice manipulating, you build up the magical muscles to use this technique to tackle the universe. Along the way you change yourself; like I said last time, you change yourself first because you don't want to change the universe and then change you and realize that that's not how you want the universe, and you have to do it again. We're all lazy buggers — I am at least, so let's do it in the right order so we don't have to do too much work. This is supposed to be fun. Does that make sense?

Now, there's a very simple exercise to develop your visualizing skills. You can do this with any object – I often use a ball point pen, so if you have a pen, you can do it with that. It's a very simple trick: you basically want to examine your physical object. It can be any physical object. Start off with something relatively simple, like that ball point pen. You want to examine it and become intimately familiar with how it looks, every individual part, and when you've got a pretty good idea of it, close your eyes, and visualize it. See it in your mind's eye, see how detailed you can get it, and then open your eyes and look at it again, and make comparisons, see the bits you missed. Check out what they look like, and try again. When you got to the point where you can see it nice and clearly, once you've got it so that you can close your eyes and picture that object absolutely clearly in detail, what I want you to do is visualize it becoming huge, the size of a spaceship. Then I want you in

Enchantment

your mind's eye to be the flying camera, and I want you to fly along the surface like you're doing a fly-by; either doing Star Trek or Star Wars across the surface of a spacecraft. I want you to fly around it, until you find a point where you can get inside it. Fly inside and fly into where the ink reservoir is and just have a good old time visualizing the thing in great detail with you being very tiny and it being very big. This is going to be homework, because I want you to do this every day. It only takes a few minutes. Pick an object, and you can use the same one every time if you want, but pick an object, have a good look at it, familiarize yourself with it, visualize it, and then do the fly-by. There is no exercise better for developing your visualization skills.

Projection Techniques

Visualizing energy as light is great way of projecting energy. Especially if you can, this is going to sound really silly, visualize the way it feels. There isn't an English word that's the equivalent for visualize for the other senses. Olfactorize? Tacticize? Develop your ability to create not just a visual image but an image with all your senses, and use that to push energy around. Now, we've all done exercises where you build a wall of energy between your hands. That's a good exercise to do, and then build a little one and practice lobbing it at people, see if they notice. Once you can project energy strongly enough that somebody else notices when they're not paying attention, the next step is to put a message into it, and that, that's one of the things we'll be doing as one of the simpler techniques of manipulation — throwing balls of intent at people.

So let's do some projecting, because it is part of the process – if you want to manipulate someone, you'd have to get your intent to where they are, and that usually is done through projecting energy. This can be done very unsubtly or it could be done very subtly. Obviously, you want to be able to do it subtly, but just like learning karate, you start with exaggerated, very unsubtle movements, and as you become more skilled you go from clumsy exaggerated moves to a simple and elegant flow.

Projecting energy is one of the practical applications of visualization because often, in order to project energy, we do it by visualizing energy as colored light, because light is energy that's visible. So if we imagine the energy that we want to move as light, we can visualize it moving. This is a very simple exercise, and once again this has got nothing to do with manipulation, but it's got everything to do with developing the muscles you need to be able to do manipulation. You need to start off by creating a ball of light, and the simplest way to do that is place your hands almost together, and see if you can feel the energy of each hand with your other hand. If you're having a problem, slap them together and rub them briskly for 30 seconds or so, and then you'll find it a lot easier. The reason for this is that you just over sensitized the nerve endings in your hand, and you could aim them at a plastic toy, and feel life force emanating from it at this point. However, that over sensitized state fades very quickly, in a matter of seconds, it is gone, but it lasted just long enough to fool your brain to stop filtering out the energy that you were sensing all along, so now you're really feeling energy. Now that you can feel the energy between your hands, start pumping more into it. Visualize your solar plexus as a reservoir of light — think of it as just white light for now — and I want you to visualize drawing that light up to your shoulders, down your arms and into the space between your hands, and I want you to create a little ball of white light. Then I want you to keep pushing the energy down your arms, feel it. In your imagination feel it pulsing down your arms, like water flowing through a faucet, and feel the pressure building between your hands. As the ball of energy grows, it should start push your hands apart slightly.

Enchantment

53

When it gets up to about the size of a baseball, I want you to squish it back down to the size of a golf ball again, and then keep on doing that, until you get a really strong feeling of energy, and then in your mind's eye you can see this glowing ball of white light. Now I want you to think of a color, a nice, bright friendly color, and I want you to change the color of the ball. To do that, start by changing the color of the reservoir, and then pushing the new color down your arms into the balls, infusing it with the color. This works for us energetically, because colors have meanings; that's why we use colored candles, that's why we use colored robes, and colored all sorts of other things, in ritual, because colors are part of a universal language: and we even use colors in descriptions – green with envy, I'm feeling blue, black rage, the red passion of love, and so on.

This next activity is a group exercise for two or more people. Join hands to form a ring of people, and then what I want you to do this time, is I want you to do the same exercise, but instead of forming the ball between your hands, I want you to build it up in your solar plexus, so rather than moving the energy from where you've got your reservoir, that is where the energy comes from, by the way, I want you to build your ball of light right there. Make it gold this time, because you're going to share it, so let's make it a nice friendly color: a nice, golden ball of light, and when you've got a golf-ball sized ball of good light that you can see clearly in your mind's eye, I want you to run it down your left arm, and then it goes through your hand into the person next to you. Meanwhile you're picking one up from the person on your right and running that up your arm, through your body, down your left arm, into the next person. So we're now passing our balls around the circle, and you feel these little gold balls traveling around the ring of people. Feel it passing, feel where everyone's kind of shifting from side to side in time with the balls. Let the balls pick up speed, and as they do, you can be a little less precise; they don't have to travel down the arm into the hand, but then up. They're just traveling from person to person now, and they're picking up speed. They're getting faster and faster, so they're not so much balls traveling now; there's a blur of gold forming a band around us. You can almost hear the hum of the energy as it builds in intensity. Silently count to 3, and on the count of 3, let go of each other's hands, and we're going to take the energy that's in our piece of the band that we've got, and we're going to throw it up in the air: One, Two, Three!

Now that can be done as a working by itself, where you fill the ball with healing energy and you aim it at somebody who isn't present to be healed directly, and you can in that way send healing to a person in another town. A lot of covens use that kind of thing, but we've looked at it a little more scientifically, looked at the raw components of it.

Now, there's a technique I've been doing for years, that is based loosely on the ancient Egyptian Mysteries, as practiced by myself, when

I was hanging around the library of the Egypt Exploration Society in London, and getting into way too much trouble, combined with some stuff that I learned from the Rosicrucians, combined with just me trying stuff out and seeing what worked, and I came up with this nifty little thing — I call it projected invocation. You can use it to push "God" energy at somebody, by invoking the god and projecting it, and it's kind of impersonal because you get the energy of the deity without the actual deity's personality. But it's useful for stuff like charging talismans or , and it's also a really good exercise for practicing projecting energy at a person to manipulate them. And once again, like the beginner at karate, it uses big, exaggerated movements, but you don't have to do once you've got the hang of it.

When I demonstrate this in a workshop, the "recipient" usually reports a sensation of being pushed back and being "charged with energy".

If I am going to project, say, Herne, I start off by visualizing the name of Herne, actually in letters, in front of me, and as I raise my hands up, I inhale it into my mouth and nasal passages. Then I exhale, and as I exhale and pushed my hands down, I multiply the word, Herne, throughout my body, going right down to the tips of my toes. Then I take a step forward, and this is the ancient Egyptian influence, the Sign of Harpocrates – there are various Deity postures that come into this bit. As I bring my hands up, I'm gathering all those many Herne names up into just behind my lips, and then as I do that — "Herne!" — I push it all out. You form a triangle between your hands, but they're not touching, and you look through the triangle, so you actually do this with your eyes rather than your hands; the hands are like the sights. Your breath and your vision is what projects the Herne energy. So you take a simple thing, a symbol or a name, and you ingest it. You multiply it throughout your body, like a virus, then you gather up those multiplied symbols or words and project them out, and the projection of energy through the eyes and with the breath is exactly the same as you do in order to manipulate others, as you will see later. It's just with manipulation, you don't flap your arms about first, because that would make people look at you funny, and then they wouldn't have a lot of respect for you at that point. You may influence people that way, but not the way you want to, that's for sure.

Peter Paddon

1.   2.   3.

4.   5.   6.

It doesn't matter how many syllables there are in the word. If you do it out loud, you sound silly no matter how many syllables there are, but really it's the force of it, rather than what you're saying and doing, that projects the power. When I first started using this technique, I used to do it out loud, which is really impressive. The first time I did it in front of other people was when I went to PEWC (Pan European Wiccan Conference), where I first met members of the Roebuck Tradition, and it's because of meeting those four people that I am now living in Los Angeles. It was in the Lake district in Britain, in England, and it was basically everyone who was anybody in the Pagan community in all of Europe, plus these crazy Americans, who got themselves invited somehow (it was an invitation-only event). I did my first ever public ritual there, an Egyptian ritual, the story of Isis and Ra, and I used this technique for proclaiming the true name of Ra. Unfortunately, the girl who was aspecting Isis in the ritual actually got temporarily blinded by that moment, and it took about 5 or 10 minutes for her to be able to see again afterwards, but I guess it worked. Anyway, I ended up in the company of some people that I had only ever read about, sitting in my hotel room afterwards, drinking wine, so I guess it impressed them a little bit, anyway. As I said, this technique is a mixture of stuff I've cobbled together from ancient Egypt, from AMORC, and from my own fetid imagination. I do that a lot, in case you haven't guessed. Some

Enchantment

of you who are into more ceremonial aspects of magick may recognize in passing the Sign of the Enterer, and the sign of Harpocrates at the end, to cut it off, the sign of silence. And the fact is that this is the magical equivalent of a karate kata. You're going through the moves because it trains the muscles, so that when you actually fight, it's bam-bam-bam, and when you actually craft or manipulate, it is a smooth flow of energy.

Now, this next exercise requires you to work with one other person. Remember the exercise where we were standing in a ring passing the energy around? Well, I want the pair of you to take each other's hands, and I want you to do the same thing, just between the two of you, and I want you to decide, one of you is the instigator. You can sit down for this, or stand, whichever you want. I want you to pick one of you to choose a color, and the other one has to try and figure out what color is being passed. This is homework, too. Do this whenever you get the chance. You may not see the person every day or you may not have somebody you can do this with every day, but when you get the chance, you decide who's going to pick the color, when that person picks the color, and the other person tries to figure out what the color is, and then when you get it right or when you give up, switch round, try it the other way. Some people are better than this than others. When you both either succeed or you've decided that you're not good with colors, try exactly the same exercise with an emotion. Keep it a simple one, keep it a pleasant one: happiness or laughter, and see if you can do it with the emotion. So start with color, when you both done the color, do an emotion, and when you've both done the emotion, I want you to do it with a word, a simple word, one syllable, keep it easy. One of the tricks with this is not to try too hard-try to keep a relaxed attitude while you do it. It doesn't matter if you get it wrong, you're doing it for practice.

Obviously, this whole thing is a lot easier to do when there's just the two of you, and if you have to practice it in a crowd of people, all making noise, it is going to make you have to work a little harder, but it's good to do that, because if you find it a little difficult here, you'll find it easier when you do it later in ideal circumstances. So don't let that bother you, it's all good practice. If you can't do this in a roomful of screaming children, then you need to do work at it.

If you find you're having a problem with a word, then pick an object and picture it as well as the word, so maybe the vision will come through easier.

Bringing About Changes in Yourself

This is about basic spell crafting. The most important work you can do right at the beginning is bringing about changes in yourself, and so I want you to start thinking –we're not going to do an actual exercise for this right now, but I want you to start thinking and making notes about this –what do you want to change about you, about your life, about your universe. Later in the book, we're going to be learning a technique that you can use to do all that. So I want you to spend some time thinking about that, so that when the time comes, you're not sitting there thinking," oh, what are we going to use this with? Oh, I know, I want, I want take-out, I want pizza". You know, if you want to manipulate the universe to bring you pizza, there's an already very effective spell you can use. It's called picking up the phone and calling Pizza Hut.

You always have to pay the coin in any spell crafting, and in this case it's a literal coin. You give them money when they bring pizza. That's not a big enough challenge.

Enchantment

Working on People and Things Remotely

What do you want to change about you, physically, emotionally, or in any other area of your life?. What do you want to improve in your life, what do you want to bring into your life? Now it's a very important part of the process, and we'll be going into more detail later. It's something that comes up in "The Secret". If you've seen the DVD of "The Secret", or read the book, you'll be interested to know that "The Secret" is right, but it's only got half the picture. What we're doing in this book is the other half of the picture, really, but one of the things they really hammer home on that DVD, and they're absolutely right to do so, is that the Universe doesn't recognize no.

The Secret... and the REAL Secret

The universe is, in fact, a drunk frat boy, and doesn't understand the word no. Do not, if you want to be debt-free, concentrate on being

Enchantment

debt-free. Do not concentrate on having no bills. Because what the universe will hear is that you're focusing on debt and bills. You need to focus on having more money. You need to couch everything in positive terms. Because whatever you're thinking of is what you'll get and if you're thinking of no-no jail time, no bills, no fear — then what you're going to get is jail time, bills and fear. Does that make sense? So while you're thinking about what you want to change in your universe, think about how you would phrase it, so it comes across as a positive statement. Now that we've set the scene, we can move on to more practical work.

Now we come to the good bit. This is the most important part of the entire book, because this is where we set things in motion, to change us, to change the universe, and to develop the skills that we're going to refine as we go through the other classes to "put the 'fluence on" people. So, as I've mentioned before, you may have watched the DVD, "The Secret", or read the book, and that's a great start because The Secret is actually pretty good. It's got about half the story, because it tells you all the wonderful things you can do but what it doesn't tell you about is all the hard work and discipline you have to use to get to the point where you can do all that. It just says that if you think really hard, you can get what you want; and to a certain extent, it's right, but if you practice and develop a discipline with the kind of stuff that is in this book, that's the missing piece, so this is what I like to call The Real Secret. "The Secret" does give us a lot of really good material, and it's actually available quite cheap now. You can buy it for about 9 or 10 dollars, not the 40-odd dollars they were selling it for, when Oprah was pushing it. It might be worth getting a copy so you can take a look, but it goes on and on, and on, repeating itself over and over and over again, in very pretty and picturesque ways.

The part that it absolutely gets right, is a pair of very important messages. The first one is that whatever you focus on, you will bring that thing into your life. The other thing is that the manner in which you focus on it is irrelevant. If you've got problems with paying the bills, and you focus on your bills with the intent of paying them, then what you will get is more bills, because you're focusing on the bills. What you need to focus on is more money, so you can pay the bills. So it's all about couching things in positive terms, because the universe doesn't understand the word "no". As I mentioned above, the universe is apparently a frat boy, and doesn't understand the word "no", so we have to couch things unambiguously, by always using terminology that is phrased in a positive way. In other words don't use phrases like "I don't want to be sick", because the part that the universe hears is sick. You do not want more "sick" in your life, not even when accompanied by "twisted". There's only so much sick and twisted we can handle at any given moment. Focus on health, focus on money coming in, focus on happiness — focus on the positive side of whatever the issue is, and that's the way to go. So that's the first secret, if you'll pardon the expression.

The next thing is also in "The Secret", and it's a fairly standard component of magick as well, that you can only do magick for something you need. A lot of people in the community in modern times, usually interpret that phrase as being well, if it's not something you really need, you shouldn't be doing magick for it, and that has it totally backwards, because it's not that you can only do magick for things that you really need; it is that in order for the magick to work you have to really feel a need to get the result. The word "need" here doesn't mean it is an essential thing, it means you need to succeed, by which I mean you have to really want it. It's like the opposite of when people read "do as thou wilt", and they interpret that as "oh, do whatever the hell you like"., but it really means "do what it is your will do to; do that what you're meant to do". Or to use the phrase made famous by Robert Cochran, "don't do what you desire, do what is necessary".

In other words, if you want to do magick for something that's a want, then you need to want it so much that it becomes a need. This is what fuels it – passion. Passion is power. Any strong emotion can fuel magick, but people who are experts can take negative emotions like hate, and sorrow, and hurt, and pain, and use them to fuel positive magick. You'll be able to do it too, but it takes practice, because when you're working with a negative emotion, you have to stop being distracted by the negative emotion. You have to transcend it and then transform it. That's how you deal with negative, powerful emotions. Those of you who have read my book, Visceral Magick, it's exactly the same thing. You will find that the powerful emotions that turn the cauldron of the heart can be positive or negative. The trick is that you have to get a positive result out of it, and, with this kind of magick, it's not always easy to work directly with the kind of emotions that are actually connected to the thing you are working

Enchantment

63

for, like "I really want this", or "I love this". You can use laughter, you can use happiness, or you can use lust. You can use any of the emotions, but if you stick with the positive ones, it's a little easier. You don't have to waste the negative ones, though – learn to use them, too, because then you transcend who you are. Instead of getting worked up by something that makes you angry, you can take that anger, and turn it into something that is positive and useful.

So passion is the name of the game. When we do these exercises to change ourselves, to manipulate other people, to change the universe, they are driven by passion. It's no good thinking along the lines of, "I'd really like to make this person sit over there, I think that would be for the best". That's not going to work. You really need to think, "it is really important, I need you to sit over there". I mean let's face it – if I was trying to convince them to get up off of their backside and move over there, saying, "I think it might be slightly better if you moved over there", they are going to say "well, I'm really comfortable where I am", but if I say "if you don't move over there, something's going to land on you and you're going to die", they are over there before you can blink, and sometimes, that's what you have to do. You have to manufacture a sense of urgency, and part of manipulating is sometimes convincing someone that blue ice from the airplane flying overhead is going to land on their seat to make them get up and move.

I have been asked by students in the past, "are there any techniques or exercises that we can use to transform the wanted result into to a need?"

The answer is, of course, that there are. First of all, ask yourself why you're doing it. The answer to that can be one of several things, but it boils down to just a handful of general options – "why am I doing this?" The answer to that is, "because if I don't, something bad is going to happen". Let that fire you up. Think about how you're preventing something bad from happening. Because we can turn "it will be really cool" into "I really need this to happen". You need to just get excited about things. If you're going to do a working to create a change in the universe, and the best you can do is well, "It'd be nice if it works", then maybe you're doing the wrong thing. Change what you're doing, and get a better result by doing something that does raise some passion in you. Then, when you are more experienced, you can take a positive emotion that is unconnected to the purpose of the magick, and re-route the resulting energy and passion.

𝕻eter 𝕻addon

64

So what I'm talking about is fueling your magick with powerful emotions. There is a very old and traditional ritual of self-improvement that is done in some of the older European magical groups. It's often referred to as the Dark Night of the Soul, though that is used as a term for other things as well. Often, approaching your initiation point is called the Dark Night of the Soul, when you encounter the Dweller on the Threshold. These are all trendy buzzwords, they're like marketing terms for wizards, but there is an older meaning to the term, Dark Night of the Soul. This is where you encounter your negativity and turn it into a positive. The ritual is difficult and unpleasant, not that normal magick is always sweetness and light. Sometimes you have to go through things that would make people run screaming, because you have to encounter the dark side of things.

So you take the negativity, and you transform it, and in the process of transforming it, you transform yourself, and while this particular old, old European ritual is difficult to achieve, the mechanics of it are actually very simple. You start off by making an incense, using things like sulfur and vinegar, and it smells bloody horrible. It doesn't really matter what you put in there, it is foul-smelling stuff. Pepper, sulfur, vinegar, turned milk, or fish heads if you want. One of my favorite passages in the Bible is actually in the Apocrypha, in the Book of Tobit, and it is the story of Tobias and the Angel. There's one part of the story of Tobias and the Angel where they're exorcising evil spirits from a house, and they make an exorcism incense, and one of the ingredients is fish heads. The instructions are, you make this incense, you take it into the house, light it, leave the house and don't go back for three days, because nothing wants to be in there for three days. It's a foul stench of exorcism, and so this ritual uses a foul stench-filled incense. It doesn't matter what it is, as long as it's unpleasant and acrid. That's why vinegar is one of the important ingredients because it makes it acrid. So you've got his nasty, acrid smoke that stings your eyes, and you basically go on a rant. You wear a rough robe, of horsehair or sack cloth, so you've got a horrible, scratchy, itchy robe. You put Mars music on, or similar, sort of strident militant music, and you stomp around and you do incantations, such as the invocation of the Bornless One..." Thee I invoke, the Bornless One –" or in the original Egyptian version, "Thee I invoke, the Headless One,. Thou that devoureth, thou that defecates upon the world and voids the universe from its fundament". These are all wonderful Revelation-esque phrases, and you basically work yourself up into a blind rage, to the point where you're almost foaming at the mouth – spittle, phlegm, you're almost incoherent with anger, and you're stomping around the temple until you are just absolutely filled with anger. Then, at that moment, when you're right on the brink of totally losing it, you have to pull it all back again, and become that calm, still center, and accept that negativity that is part of you. It is your own shadow self, and you accept it into you, because it's you — you can't reject it, so you acknowledge it, because only by acknowledging and accepting that which is negative within you can you transform it.

You embrace it, and you draw the calmness, that still center around it, and what it does is, it makes you incredibly powerful. You won't find many people teaching that particular ritual. I mean it's not like there's a script for it anyway. You have to build it personally, but I can't think of any magical order that I'm aware of in the current day and age that actually do that kind of ritual, yet it used to be a standard part of your spiritual evolution. That is passion. Sex magick works, because it builds passion – it is popular because it is sex magick. For a lot of people who say "oh, yes, I'm a sex magician", what they mean is "I dress up in robes and have sex, and it's pretty magical". Really what you're looking at with sex magick is you're building up the passion again, the passion and the lust and the power and the potency. The hard part for most of us, if you'll pardon the expression, the other hard part for most of us, is then actually maintaining focus to direct all that power and passion. Real sex magick is not about pleasure, because you take all the fun out of it by having to focus on the outcome of the ritual. Real sex magick is not sex, it is magick that involved bodily functions. It's not fun. Well, a little bit fun. It is fun to practice.

One-Point Concentration and the Quartz Crystal

Now when it comes to working on manipulating other people, yourself and the universe, you need to be able to develop what is often called single point focus. It's sometimes called tunnel vision in sports, where the world goes black except for that little pin prick right in front of you that is the focus of your attention. I know a lot of marksmen get tunnel vision when they shoot – I do. You focus so much on the target that the rest of the world goes away; it can happen to sword fighters as well. I remember one particular time because I used to shoot, and I used to sword fight, and I used to dance. I remember one particular sword fight, this young lad, Craig, had just joined the Renaissance guild that we were members of, and he was a competitive fencer. This is the first time we met the guy, and I got to have a sword fight with him. We were using broadswords, and I actually went and borrowed a lighter broadsword from someone else so I could keep up with him, because he was really fast, and what started out being just a simple sparring session, turned out to be a ritual all by itself. He was so good and he stretched my abilities, and we got into that Zen moment where instead of being a sword fight, it became a dance, and I actually found myself "watching" the two of us from about 10 feet away, performing this ritual with the swords. It was just absolutely magical, absolutely beautiful. It's the most sublime sword fighting experience I've ever had in my life. That is magick. That is single focus, single point focus, and that's what we're going to learn to do now, because it's the key to everything. This is the key that unlocks the secret door to world domination, or just being able to manipulate things.

This is where the crystal comes in handy. Now don't laugh, but after making a big fuss about the need for a quartz crystal pebble, you don't actually need it. However, using the crystal makes it easier and makes you get results faster, so why not use it, and save yourself some time? It's not one of those things where if you use the crystal you'll never be able to do it without a crystal – no, it doesn't work that way. By using the crystal you'll develop the ability quicker and faster, and better, than you would without it. Then if you want to, you can throw the crystal away. You probably won't because it will still make it faster – doing it with the crystal is always faster than doing it without. You may wonder, "does it have to be a quartz crystal?" I made a point of describing quartz crystal pebbles – nice and smooth, reasonably clear, a quartz crystal. Why did I do that? Because you don't have to, in a pinch you could use a bottle of water — take the label off, and use that. But if the thing that you use is always the same, it will become easier and faster to use it, because it takes on something of you, something of your energy. It's like the way that a master craftsman always works better with his own tools – not because the tools are inherently special, but because a master craftsman knows his tools. He knows the feel of them in his hands. He knows how they're going to behave, he knows their little quirks. He knows that that saw has a bent tooth, that if he draws too far, he's going to get a mark, that it is going to make a mess of what he's doing. So he takes shorter strokes, because he really likes that saw, but he has to allow for its imperfections. By using the same tool every time, you develop a symbiosis with it, and the same applies to the crystal.

So how do we use it? Well, it's very, very simple. You can actually use anything shiny or anything that light can pass through or reflect off — you could use a scrunched up candy wrapper. The thing is, it's got to be something that can get your attention, and quartz crystal is really good at catching light, and the technique we're going to use is almost identical to the technique you use when you are skrying with a crystal ball, just on a smaller scale. As I've told many of my students in the past, you can actually buy a small crystal ball to use for this particular task, but pebbles are a lot cheaper.

You will want to have a dark background behind your crystal, so place it on the pouch, that's why I specified a black pouch. Now, ideally, you're going to do this by yourself without anyone else around, and you will want to do it in dim light. I don't mean like when you're doing the energy around the hand thing, I mean you don't want to have bright lights. What you are looking for is soft, indirect light, and you don't want to have any lights shining directly on you. Ultimately, you should be able to do this any time, day or night, but it's easier at first to do it in indirect light, a gray day is just the right lighting. It really is a very simple exercise, one that can be done sitting or standing – it's easier to do sitting, but I often prefer to do it standing, so you can do it standing as well. Ideally, you don't want too many distractions. So what you're basically going to do is you're just going to gaze at the crystal — by gaze, I mean don't focus your eyes on it. You don't want to look at it in sharp relief like you did with the pen other object in the visualization exercise earlier in this book. You almost want to gaze past it. Focus on the cloth that it's resting on. It helps if you're looking down at it, because you can kind of cup your hand, or cup the bag, and stop any direct light from shining on it. You kind of want a kind of cloudiness to develop inside it, and if you're looking at it out of focus, you'll find that it really does kind of cloud up after a while. Now at no point do you need to see anything in the crystal. The visualization takes place up within your heart and your mind. If you do project the image into the crystal, that's fine, too, but you don't have to.

So you just basically focus your attention on the crystal, because it's shiny and sparkly and it's intriguing, and with the nature of quartz being what it is, it's very easy to focus on. It isn't so easy to focus if you have a lot of distractions, not at first, but by yourself you'll find it very easy to just make the world go away and get into that "now" moment with it. So it puts you in trance, and it opens up the faculties for the desired visualization, it promotes the visualization process. Now you're going to do other things with this crystal as we learn more about manipulation, but this is the basic exercise that is the heart and soul of this whole process. Let yourself just gaze gently at the stone, and when you're doing this by yourself, you'll do it for about five minutes. No more, just five minutes. At some point, you will feel yourself getting into that "now" space –and it's really easy to tell because things seem to slow down and the air seems to get a little thicker, and you just feel like time has stopped. It's almost like the clock hand goes tick... tick... and then stops. And that's the point, when there's this calm nothingness around you, and within you, that you begin to visualize, and you visualize the thing you want to bring about, the thing you want to change. You want a better job – visualize it, see it. You want more money coming in, you want more health, you want to get fit, you want a friend, a lover, to find long-lost family members, you want to be able to explore, you want to do something you've never done before – picture it, picture yourself doing that thing... finding that thing... getting that thing... becoming that thing.

Visualize it, see it in your mind's eye as clearly and as strongly and as powerfully as you can. Let it evoke emotions, so you feel the wanting, the need for that thing. For some people, it works better if the image moves, if you can see yourself actually doing something, or see whomever you're aiming it at doing something, doing the thing you want them to do, in motion. For other people, a static image works best. Play with it, and find out what works best for you. The trick is to get so focused on it and so invested in it that for a moment, it becomes real to you for just a fraction of an instant. It's as if it has already happened, and

Enchantment

for a moment, you believe that it's happened, that it's come about, that it's done, and at that point, you can relax, say thank you to the universe, or whatever entities you work with in your practice, and go about your business. Start doing it for five minutes every day, pick something to do. You could do the same thing every day or you can do a different thing every day, but do it for five minutes. Then, when you start to feel it working, extend the time. Don't ever do the visualizations for longer than an hour, because that's just a waste of time, but see if you can extend it within that limit, because it develops your focus, and it develops those muscles.

Altering Reality

So how does this help us manipulate people? Well, for one thing, you can manipulate people from a distance, just by doing this. You want somebody who is really pissing you off at work to go away, for example. Remember, be positive, couch things in positive terms. So you want them to go away: you want them to find a wonderful opportunity that they can't resist, a better job, a better life, more money and happiness, and it's the other side of the country. Give them something good that makes them go where you want them to go – away. It is much better this way, if you believe in Karma, because it stops the karmic fallout from kicking you in the butt afterwards, because you've done something nice for them — that happens to benefit you. I'm very fond of that approach. So keep it positive.

Start with simple little things: things that you can validate. Try and bring about a change, like somebody who is always grumpy when you go into work in the mornings. Try and make them greet you with a smile, and see how long it takes you to achieve that. Then pick another similar thing, a simple easy thing, and see if you can do it sooner, then try something a little more difficult and see how quickly you do that. You know, it's like weight training – you start easy and light and you build the muscles up, and then you try bigger and better things. This technique will work for you and keep growing for you for the rest of your life as long as you keep doing it. It does seem really simple and silly — I've asked you to buy a $1 and a half — $2 crystal pebble and gaze at it. Yes, you can blink — don't try and not blink, because that will totally blow your focus. No, just gently relax. Remember, don't try too hard, just sit or stand and relax, and when you need to blink, blink.

Peter Paddon

You'll find you blink less often because as you go into trance, everything slows down and your rate of blinking will get slower and slower. So don't worry about it, don't think about it. Just let it happen as if it were the most natural thing in the world. This technique is the most important technique you're going to learn in this entire book.

A student asked me, "Do you recommend that we try it on somebody else, or should the change we want to accomplish be for ourselves from within?"

My answer to this question is simple: Start with yourself, but once you've done one or two for yourself, try doing one that affects somebody else. Alternate the target, be creative, be diverse, because at some point, as you start to get successes, you will begin to realize some of the applications you could use this for. Remember, the only thing separating success from failure with this technique is practice. If you do it once and it doesn't work and you don't bother for a week, and then you try again, you're going to be back at square one. If you do it every day, you're going to get better at it. When you want to change things in yourself, start with the little things like "I want to get up earlier in the morning, so that I can exercise or eat a healthy breakfast, or have time to pick the clothes I wear before I throw them on and go to work". Start with little things like that, and then "I want a more challenging job, a more interesting job, a job that pays better — I want a promotion". You will need to practice a lot, in order to get really good, but there's no reason why you couldn't become an expert, because this is the core technique. This technique will enable you to do that great thing that Archimedes described – "Give me a lever long enough and a fulcrum on which to place it, and I shall move the world." This is your fulcrum point; the lever is your focus, and your passion. You can move the Earth, literally. You can make the universe conform to your needs, because let's face it – as magical people, you are at the center of your universe, subjectively speaking, and this technique with the fulcrum point; this is the point of stillness in the universe and energy to move everything else. It is one of the reasons why it is important for you to use the same crystal each time, and not let anyone else it.

You may find that as you develop your focusing abilities and being able to gaze gently at it, you'll get a sensation of falling into the crystal. This is not unusual. People who use crystal balls for fortune telling often say that this is the point they know they're getting good at it, because the crystal draws you in. You become drawn to the focal point, and you experience that as a sensation of "falling in". It's really cool when it happens — I can guarantee that each and every one of you, the first time it happens, will let out a scream that can be heard from across town, because it is that cool, it really is. Now, this technique with the crystal has been around for a long time. It's one of those "hidden in plain sight" kind of things, and it's often called a seeing stone, or a show stone. Back in the Elizabethan days, they called it a shew stone, S-H-E-W, which rhymes with sew. John Dee had one — you all know who John Dee is? John Dee, the court astrologer to Queen Elizabeth the first. He was the creator — or discoverer, depending on your perspective — of the Enochian magical system, a form of Angelic magick. He was a secret agent – possibly the first — code-named 007; he was a spy for the queen. He was also one of the last great Renaissance men. Not in the sense that he lived in the Renaissance period (though he did), but he was a Renaissance man in the sense he was considered to be someone who contained within him the sum of human knowledge. After him, there was too much of it to cram into one skull, so we can't do that anymore. We can still get a Renaissance man who becomes the master of many practices, for want of a better description. So the term shew stone has been around for a long time. Aleister Crowley chose to use a shew stone to do his calls to the Enochian Aethers. He's one of the few people on record to have worked with all of the 30 Aethers of the Enochian magick system. Some people would say not all of him came back from them. Once again, it's a matter of perspective, but the shew stone used to be part of the Renaissance magician's tools of the trade.

So how do you use the crystal to change yourself? Well, hopefully that's pretty straightforward. At least at the beginning, because you'll think I want to lose weight, I want to get healthy, start with the simple stuff then work up. You change it into a need by becoming passionate about it, so when you go through your list and you pick one that you want to focus on, that's when you inject the "need" into it and put the passion into it. To start off, make it easy for yourself, pick things that you're already passionate about, such as building the perfect model railway layout (one student in the workshops is passionate about this), then you've just got to manifest it. Use your crystal to manifest it, and you walk into the model railway store, and they have just the right pieces you need.

The universe doesn't often make things appear in a flash of light in front of you — it does happen, I've seen it happen, so I know it does, but it's kind of scary when it happens, so it's a good job it doesn't happen too often. I used to have a stone very similar to the one we're using for manipulation, that I did some very nefarious magick work on back in1991 or 1992, when I was back in England, many years ago. My first wife — we were still married at this point -was going to Egypt, but I couldn't go with her because I had exams for a management course I was taking scheduled the same week. I'd already been a year or so before, but I didn't go that time. She was also going to be gone on my birthday, which is January 11th of that particular year, which was the year that the New Age "11:11" thing was supposed to happen, which was supposedly some big cosmic gate opening in Egypt.

So I got 13 assorted little crystal pebbles, amethyst, garnets, carnelians and lapis lazuli, and I had one big clear quartz crystal. That was the 13th rock. I worked on linking all those little stones to the quartz crystal, and I kept the quartz crystal and gave my wife the other 12, and said "while you're in Egypt, drop one of these in the sanctuary of a different temple", and she did. So, at 11:11 AM on January the 11th, on my birthday, I sat there in my temple with the quartz crystal in my hand, and reestablished my connection with the other 12 stones, that by this time had all been placed, tucked in a nook or a cranny, in the sanctuary of one of the big temples in Egypt: The Temple of Osiris at Abydos, the Temple of Hathor at Denderah, the Temple of Isis at Philae, the Mortuary temple of Queen Hatshepsut, the Mortuary temple of Ramses the Great. She'd even flicked one of them into the Osirion, behind the Temple of Abydos. It is the actual, original cult center of the Cult of Osiris and Wepwawet, who became merged with Anubis. It's the oldest temple in Egypt, and there is a symbol burned on the wall that's become known as the Flower of Life. Nobody knows how it got burned on there, it is like it was laser-burned on the wall, but it's somewhere in the region of 10,000 years old. So she even managed to get one of the stones in there, because it's half submerged and you can't go in, there's an iron gate, bars, and she flicked a stone through it. It's only a little temple.

Enchantment

That stone was the most incredible healing tool I've ever had. I used to carry it around in my pocket, and every night I'd place it on my bedside table, but about once a month I'd get up and it would be gone. Three days later it would be back – on the third morning it would be back on the bedside table. Then, one day it just went away, and never came back again. So yes, things can physically manifest (known as an apport) and disappear, but don't expect that. Rather, if you decide to do a working for a rare book that you want for your studies, don't expect to wake up the next morning and find it at the foot of your bed. Expect Great Aunt Bertha to find a copy at a used book store and get it for your birthday. Or expect to find it in a used book store yourself, next time you go to a used bookstore. It'll come to you through mundane means, but it will come to you. So have fun with that.

So how do we change the universe? Well, that's really simple. Every time you do magick you change the universe, because that's the way magick works. You have your sacred space, even if you're just doing a little crafting by yourself at the kitchen counter, you create sacred space around yourself, magical space; that little enclosure, that little circle, that little ball of energy that's just yours. It basically consists of a sphere of energy around a point of stillness. That stillness is the fulcrum, and the sphere, this magick circle if you will, is a bit like a gyroscope. It balances on the fulcrum point, and no matter what you do, it stays balanced, but think about those gyroscope toys we all had as a kid – how did we make it move? If it was perfectly balanced, it stayed put, but if you tipped it, it would shift until it regained its equilibrium. When we do magick, when we do spells, when we do crafting, that's what we're doing. We create an imbalance in the energy, and because it's gyroscopic, it's spinning, the center moves until it rights itself, and at that point it takes the universe with it. It moves the universe, to correct the imbalance. To put it in more direct terms, there is an absence of this thing that I want, and I really want it, so there's this need creating an imbalance. The universe moves to correct that imbalance, and in doing so it brings about the thing that I am working for. So even when you work for the little things, like a book, or a job, or to get that person in the office to smile at you tomorrow morning when you go in, instead of bitching and moaning about cold coffee, you move the entire universe into a position where that can happen. So when you actually want to move the universe, you just do exactly the same thing. You just you have a bigger end result than before. You want to change the universe, you want to make politicians more reasonable – well, good luck with that. All things are possible, but some might just be more effort than it is worth! Moving the universe is easy, but recognizing what you want it to do when it gets there, that's the hard part.

So how do you use the crystal to change others? Well, instead of focusing on you doing something, you focus on them doing something, or being something, or becoming something, or receiving something. You couch it in positive terms, and you put passion behind it. Believe for an instant it's already happened, because that seals the deal, that grounds it in reality. Because you, me, each of us, we don't see reality; we see the universe through a filter, or a series of filters, of our own beliefs and expectations. We get what we expect from the universe. That really puts it into perspective. If you've got a crappy life, it's because you expect a crappy life. A lot of people get morally offended if you say to them "bad things in your life come to you because you called them to yourself". The response is often along the lines of "I didn't ask to be sick", "I didn't ask for a life of solitude fueled only by multiple cats", "I didn't ask for this, I didn't ask to be a nerd or a dweeb or, or a social outcast". Well, the theory is that some part of you felt you needed to do that — some part of you felt that this was a part of your process: but that doesn't mean you can't turn around and say "okay, I'm done with that now. Let's move on to the next thing". The trick is, just because illness or sorrow or loss or pain comes into your life, doesn't mean that it has to stay there. "So, this thing has come into my life; I have obviously called it. Obviously there was a need for it in my life at some point, some lesson to learn from it. I get it. Let's move on to the next step". Cure yourself, heal yourself, turn yourself around, change your life, change the universe. It really is that simple. The hard part is that you have to believe in yourself, and that's why I said, right at the beginning, that one of the important things here is that you have to be confident in yourself.

So part of this process with the homework and doing these things daily, is to build up your confidence. You need to learn to believe in "you", and for some people, that's the hardest part of the whole process. You need to learn to believe in yourself, because you are magnificent,

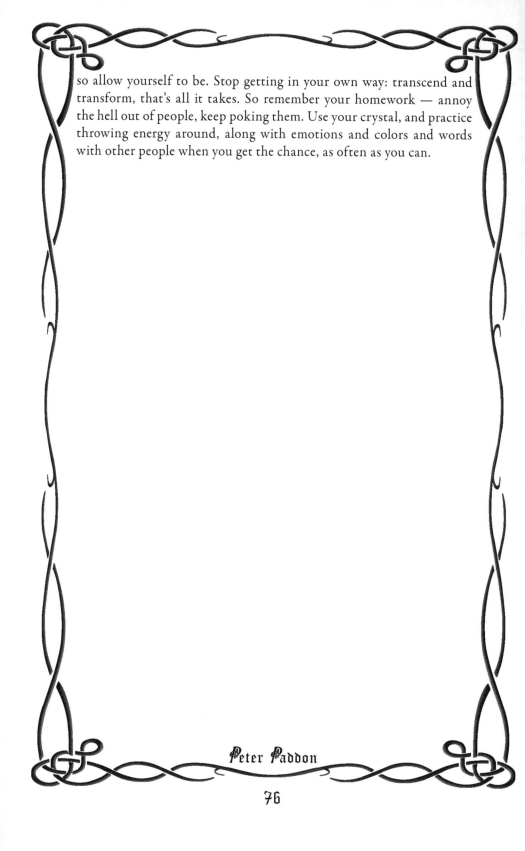

so allow yourself to be. Stop getting in your own way: transcend and transform, that's all it takes. So remember your homework — annoy the hell out of people, keep poking them. Use your crystal, and practice throwing energy around, along with emotions and colors and words with other people when you get the chance, as often as you can.

Peter Paddon

Direct Manipulation Through Touch

So this is the chapter you've been waiting for. This is where we learn the actual techniques of enchantment, because it's all really very simple. The secret is in practicing, doing it over and over and over again. Now I hope you have been playing with your crystal, and that you've been getting some results. I know that a lot of the people in my experimental workshop used their crystal to get hotel rooms in the room lottery for PantheaCon, the main Pagan event on the West Coast, and I helped my son get a good job by using my crystal. Now, none of the exercises we do in this section involve the crystal. The crystal is the equivalent of you going to the gym. The crystal is a tool that builds up the muscles that we need, to do the stuff you're going to learn next, but you don't actually use the crystal for these exercises. However, the crystal exercise is a practical exercise for changing the universe, as you may or may not have already discovered, so keep using it. I do have to confess to one little piece of trickery. I went on about everyone buying a quartz crystal

Enchantment

pebble for this, because it is the simplest and easiest tool to use for the job. This is your "training wheels", because you will find as you practice with your crystal pebble that sooner or later, the crystal that you're meant to use for the rest of your life will make itself known to you, and you will have to get it. Now, that crystal may not be a quartz crystal pebble. For example, the one that made itself known to me — and it's still quartz – is a beautiful faceted single point crystal I found that if I hold it in my hand, wrapped by my fingers, so I've got the flat base towards me and I use it like the end of a telescope, it's really cool and really potent, and now I can't even pick up the pebble I was using. It's become useless to me, because this is the one I'm meant to use.

So the crystal pebble is there to get you to this point, where the universe thinks that you need something a bit better, and goes, "here, have this", and then off you go with the new one. So I thought I'd give you a heads-up about that, so you won't be surprised when suddenly, you find yourself with a jagged piece of obsidian in your hand going, "oh, I absolutely need to be using this!" Well, some of us have that problem with any rock, it seems to be part of being magical that we are attracted to rocks and crystals in general: but you know what I mean.

Voluntary Trance-Inducing Touch Techniques

So now we are going to talk about direct manipulation through touch, because that's the easiest way to manipulate someone else. When you have physical contact with the person you're trying to manipulate, it's a lot easier, because you haven't got to build up your energy and throw it at them.

First of all, there are the voluntary trance-inducing touch techniques, which are designed for working with a willing partner, in order to develop your skill and confidence. This begins with putting yourself in a light trance, using some of the techniques we've already explored, but I'm going to revisit them briefly because I want you to play with them; so to start off with, let's do the solo one, which is the lifting your own skull. Ok, so you start off by putting your chin down, putting it forward, lifting it up, and then gazing slightly above the horizon, so your chin is slightly higher than it would have been for normal conversational purposes. You then just feel the way that makes you feel, and relax. Hopefully you are quite good at that by now.

Ok. Next, I want you to try inducing a trance in a willing partner. Stand up — you can do this in front or behind of your partner, but the very simple

technique to induce trance consists of stroking their upper arms in a downward motion. That's all it takes, and as I mentioned earlier, if you've got a baby that won't go to sleep, doing a variation of this on the baby's forehead, down the bridge of the nose works really well. But with an adult subject, the arms work nicely, and the subject will quite quickly begin to feel nice and dreamy. So with your partner, see how dreamy you can make them feel. Incidentally, this is why you should always tell your daughters never to let the young lads get their hands on them, as this is an old "player" technique to make a young girl compliant and less likely to resist the amorous advances of her "Romeo"

Enchantment

Another way of doing this will be familiar to fans of Star Trek, because it's very similar to the Vulcan Mind Meld. Surprisingly, there is a real thing that works this way. Now you don't have to go to the points that Spock used, all you need to do once again is physical contact. I find you can use one or both hands, you can do this on one side or both sides, as long as you've got a finger on the temple and a finger on the jaw, and your thumb somewhere around the back of the head – that's enough. What you do then is you just send waves of calm, relaxing energy. You'll be surprised how effective that can be. This is really, really simple — just remember the visualization techniques we did previously. You just see gentle, golden light. I find gold actually works best for this – a nice muted antique gold works really well for this exercise. You can use other colors, but they need to be gentle and relaxing, and gold seems to work with everyone.

It's amazing how simple these exercises are when you consider that it's something that people poo-poo as not really being real. It really does work very quickly, very simply. Now, with this particular one, if you can avoid

Peter Paddon

them pushing your hand away, you can actually use it on somebody against their will this way, but you have to be quick and practiced. To reiterate the technique, you want to have roughly one finger somewhere around the temple — it is best if you do use your index finger there, because you want to have a finger down as close to the jawline as you can, such your little finger, and then your thumb around the back of the head. It just gives you a spread, which seems to increase the effectiveness. There'll be lots of philosophical and religious reasons you can come up with for this.

Involuntary Trance-Inducing Touch Techniques

So now we come to involuntary trance inducing techniques. Because let's face it, 99% of the time when you want to manipulate somebody, they're not actually going to be a willing victim, unless it's kinky bedroom games, in which case, have at it. You can stroke anything you like at that point.

To begin with, the thing with physical contact with someone who doesn't want to be manipulated by you is that obviously there's a certain level of subterfuge and subtlety involved. You can't go up to somebody and make dramatic gestures as you grab them because they'll be calling the Police. So you have to make use of much more mundane connections, and the first of these, is very simple. "Pleased to meet you" — hand to

Enchantment

hand contact under the pretense of a handshake. It's not quite as simple as that, obviously, because what you want to do is to focus on, once again, your thumb and index finger, so they're sort of across from each other, so there's a nice cross section of hand between them. That way, you can zap in, and it's like a human Taser. I'm going to talk about the specifics of the visualization energy work after I've described physical techniques, but basically you're doing the same thing you did with the "Spock mind meld", only you're doing it with the hands. "Pleased to meet you" – try it with your partner, and see if they feel the effect: in the workshops we definitely got some strong results from this one.

That's basically exactly the same technique as the mind meld. It helps if you can get somewhere near the pulse point, though it isn't essential to be right on the pulse point, but just somewhere near it. There's a nerve plexus in there as well, one that modern-day Ninjas use to cripple you with a ballpoint pen or a stick (using pressure-point techniques). However, you don't want to cause pain; you're just using those as access points. In a way you are using the pulse/pressure point as a way to "plug in" to your victim's "circuitry", and once you've got that, it is about the strongest physical connection you can get, and then you are basically just shooting your manipulation straight up their arm. Of course, for the purposes of this exercise, we're just looking for a relaxed trance state. Once you've got the 'fluence flowing, you can actually provide a little bit of movement, using a small circular motion with the tip of your thumb or index finger, which makes a significant difference to the results. Believe it or not, the hand is an incredibly sensitive instrument, especially in this soft fleshy area around the pulse point. I used to do a little trick back in my younger days, to see how many pretty girls I could get their knees to buckle, just by kissing there. Right there, over the pulse point, is one of the most erogenous zones in the body, that and the back of the knees, but this one's easier to get

to. So remember, it's exactly the same technique you used with the mind meld; you're just doing it hand to hand. In a pinch, you can do it fingertip to fingertip, but if you can get it in the ideal position, why not maximize the efficiency?

Here's an important safety tip — don't try too hard. Go gently, and build it up if you need to, because you can put quite a jolt through people if you're not careful. When your partner is feeling the effect, try rotating the tip of your thumb on the spot where it rests and see what difference that makes.

You can do the same thing just by any physical contact at any random point in the body. It needs a little more practice, though: it will take some practice to be able to do that without a nerve or pulse point where you are touching them, but to be honest, it's mostly confidence that makes it work, and that's why I'm teaching you the ones that are easy to do first, with a direct connection to the person's energy flow, because it gives you confidence. When you see it works, when you feel

Enchantment

83

it works, you then have more confidence when you try the next one, that's a little bit trickier. So once again, it is important to practice these exercises until they become second nature. Whenever you get the opportunity, do some practice with the "Spock", the handshake, and the arm rub to build up your confidence, and build up your familiarity with the way it feels. Then try switching over to just as you walk past the person, your test subject, your willing victim, just put your hand on their shoulder as you walk past them and see if you can get them to get drawn in just in that brief touch.

Obviously, it's much easier if you have a willing partner to practice with, but the handshake one doesn't have to involve a willing victim. In fact, once you've done it with a willing partner – you'll want to go out and find a complete stranger, but remember, make sure you are being ethical, even if messing with strangers can be somewhat naughty.

One of the workshop students asked me what to do if the unsuspecting victim does the handshake thing back at you...well, one of the cool things about all this is, if you know this technique and you feel it being done back at you, you can use the technique to block it, to counteract it. So you can make yourself impervious to other people's influence, using the very same technique.

Projecting Energy and Imagery through Touch

Okay, so let's talk about projecting energy and imagery through touch. What we have been doing in the exercises so far has been just to relax and get people into their trance state, which makes them easier to manipulate. It makes them more suggestible, to use the term from hypnotism — even though this isn't really hypnotism. So what you then want to do is move on to the next stage. Manipulation isn't usually about making someone feel drowsy — you want them to do something for you, or give you information or, you know, whatever nefarious scheme you're up to. How do we get the command into the structure? It really is quite simply that you talk to them – not with your mouth, though — but it has to be as forceful as if you were speaking – the way I speak when I'm teaching a class, it isn't my everyday voice, my sitting on the couch watching TV and muttering inanities to my wife voice; this is my talking to a bunch of people in a room voice. You know? That's the voice you need to use, but without any sound, which means keeping the mouth muscles still as well, because you'll give the game away if your mouth is moving. Or they'll think you're a lunatic, and they won't let you touch them. That kind of spoils all the fun. Very simply, the old-fashioned way of describing this is to say it strongly in your mind, not with your mouth. Always use positive phrases — we've covered this in the first chapter, that the universe doesn't understand the word "no". So you don't tell them to not do something; tell them to do the thing you want them to do. In other words, if you want them to not go to work the next day, tell them to stay at home. That's what I mean by a positive statement. Don't use phrases that have the words no, not, never, or anything negative in them. Always phrase it positively. So if you want the bouncer at the nightclub door to let you in, even though you're not on the list, tell him that you want to go in. Tell him to let you in, tell him you're on the list. One of the participants of the workshops got let in through the VIP entrance to a convention even though she wasn't on the list, because she was in a hurry — twice — and got to park where no one was allowed to park.

You need to feel the force of what you are silently saying. It is the power of the unspoken word, to use the classic terminology. So you've got to put a lot of mental effort into this, and you're going to see the energy flow as a wave, down your arm, or your arms, into the person. Above all you've got to be confident; that's why we do the exercises leading up to this; primarily, because it's confidence that powers the whole process. If you doubt yourself, you will short circuit the process — it's really as simple as that. So build up your confidence with the basic exercise, and then

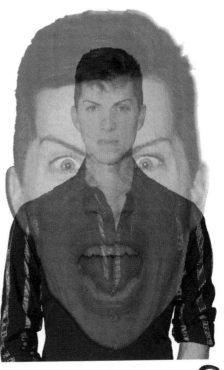

Enchantment

introduce simple commands. It's like training a dog, really. See your thoughts as a wave of light energy. Actually, try to involve as many of your senses as you can — feel the energy, try and visualize it, see it as a light or a sort of motion blur or something, and it should be at the most forceful right at the end. So you kind of push it, push it, then shove.... and then take your hand away.

For the purposes of demonstration, let's say your partner is a woman, and you are going to get her to turn one way or the other. Obviously she's a willing victim, so she's going to cooperate with you, but you are not going to tell her in advance which way you want her to turn. So the first thing you do is make a contact, and let the energy flow. Then you say your phrase, silently, and push the instruction to her. She should feel the urge to turn in the direction you want her to, and with a little practice, she will simply turn.

The woman with whom I demonstrated this exercise in the workshop described what she felt as, "there was a — even though your hand was there, there was like a pushing sensation, like it was my whole side, so I was like, no, I want to resist that. Did you see me kind of try to go the other way? And I couldn't, I needed to go that way. But it went all the way down to my buttocks, and then just kind of pushed me this way."

Peter Paddon

To be honest, that demonstration wasn't a lot of effort, and I'm not a great expert at this. I had been practicing this about as much as you hopefully have by now. I learned a lot of this stuff years ago, and hadn't used it since, but teaching the workshops was an excuse to brush the cobwebs off it, and try it out again, to take it for a test drive. So, there wasn't a lot of power behind that demonstration, but she felt it as a real, physical thing. When you are trying this exercise, if you can visualize the turning rather than putting it into words, it'll probably work much better.

Manipulation through Gesture

Everything we're doing now is just building on exactly the same techniques, but taking it one step further. So you started off with the "grip of death" on your willing victim, and moved on to much more subtle physical contact. Now we let go of our victim, and make use of what are traditionally known as magnetic passes.

Magnetic Passes

Magnetic passes are very simple — there are three basic forms of magnetic passes. The first one is regular monotonous circular motions with the hand, and if you've watched the Jedi mind trick gestures in the Star Wars movies, that is exactly what we're talking about, especially if you get up in someone's face with it. If you get close enough to somebody that you can basically do this half-way between you and them, their eyes will almost involuntarily watch your fingertips, and that circular motion, guess what? It puts them in trance.

Enchantment

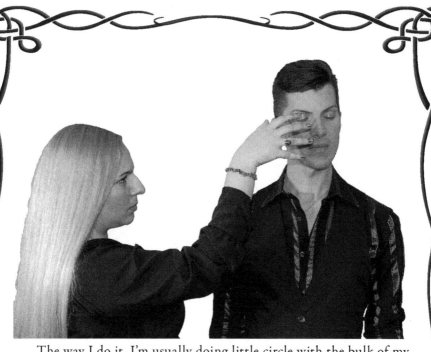

The way I do it, I'm usually doing little circle with the bulk of my hand, while my fingertips are doing a bigger circle. So if I hold the palm of my hand still, my fingers are drawing circles in the air, and then I'm adding the circular motion of the wrist to that initial movement. Imagine stroking an invisible cat that's floating in the air in front of you. Make your movements smooth and slow, flowing gracefully, as you want to invoke a smooth flowing movement of the victim's eyes, without any jarring or jerkiness.

The second gesture, the second magnetic pass, is a wavelike motion up and down, with the emphasis on the down. You're not break dancing, but you do this sort of wave motion with the emphasis on the down. Down, up. Down, up. So as you go down, extend your fingers; as you go up, let them curl in, and you'll understand the difference when you actually do the physical motion.

Peter Paddon

The third kind of motion is a drawing in, like you're sampling the fragrance of a good incense smoke. So if you think of literally wafting the incense towards you, and then lower your hands down so you're "wafting" towards your heart, drawing them in.

Inducing Trance through Passes

You can use these passes to induce trance in your victim — you can use any of the different passes but, to begin with it's probably easiest if you use the wave. You'll realize at once that this is not something you can do to a stranger, because they'll wonder what the hell's going on from the get-go, but this exercise is, once again, a means to an end. So you start off by doing passes down, and then when you feel it taking effect, change to the circular pass in front of the face, and then down the arms. Once again, this isn't taking a lot of mental effort, and it's not taking a lot of physical effort. Then you take their hands, and look them in the eye, and just in your mind say the command phrase you have chosen, and then you can let go of their hand, but keep the eye contact. A good exercise to practice this with is to attempt to draw your "victim" towards you. Begin by standing a few feet in front them. Start putting the 'fluence on her with the passes, in front of you. Use big downward motions — you do one or two hands — and when you feel there's a connection there, switch to the circular passes in front of their face. Then make passes down, down the sides, along their arms, and then take their hands and fix your gaze on theirs. Will them to relax. Then let go of their hands, and then draw them towards you. Try to pull them in until they lose balance.

The really cool thing is that once you know what it feels like, it's going to be almost impossible for someone to do it to you, because you'll feel it coming, and will be able to use the same energetic work to cancel it out. Your own familiarity with the technique, your expertise, will enable you to prevent entering into the passive, receptive trance that makes the whole thing so effective. You have the edge there, but because they have not been trained in the technique, they will be in the trance state before they are aware that anything is going on, and will not be able to resist. That's the reason why the trance thing is useful, at least at the beginning. When you get good at this, you won't need to do the trance. You can just go straight to the manipulation, but the trance gives you an edge when you're learning which helps build your confidence. It's like the trance part is the training wheels

So obviously, you can cause them to sway, you can cause them to turn; you can drag them around the room. When you're practicing at home, see if you can get your test subject to move around the available space. Because once you've gotten to that point, you don't have to be physically close to them. As long as you can keep within what you feel is your range – your range will increase with exercise and practice, so have them move around the room.

I was asked about whether this would work on someone with ADHD, and I don't really have any experience with that, but some of the students in my workshops assured me that it does, indeed, work on people with ADHD as well.

You can use this in very subtle ways. Now, you might think that moving people around isn't good for much other than as a party trick. Well, you'd be amazed at how many decisions you can change based on where someone is standing. Someone reaches to press a button, and you cause them to press the one next to it, so instead of voting yes, they vote no.

Manipulating Energy through Passes

It isn't just people you can influence with these passes. Just as physical gestures can alter the flow of smoke from incense, so these passes can influence the flow of energy in crafting or ritual. By keeping your movements graceful and flowing, you can use these same passes to redirect and amplify the flow of energy.

The Art of the "Puppet-Master"

With practice, you can make people move like you were a puppet master — you physically manipulate your subjects into doing simple things. For example, if you're trying to choose between two dishes at a buffet, but there's one left of the one you like, and the person in front of you is heading towards it, put the 'fluence on them. Turn them just a little bit, so they see the other option, and go for that instead, and the one you want is left untouched. Little things like that can be very effective; it's amazing how much we can manipulate someone just by changing where they're looking. Sometimes, half the problem is making people see something in the first place, so they can choose it.

One of the students at the workshop asked me if this will work on animals too, and the answer is that yes, it will work if you are the kind of person who has a rapport with animals, if you can naturally connect with them... in other words, if you are already an "animal person". Of course, you probably want to work more on images than

words in that case. It is easier to tell with some animals than others —
with a reptile, you might have to "plant a seed" that comes to fruition
sometime later, and in the meantime, they just sit there, with no
indication that they have received your manipulation.

Direct Manipulation through Gaze

The Power of the Gaze

You'll notice in the last exercise, when we were doing the passes, that the gaze actually plays an important part, because you basically use the gesture to draw them and to get them in trance, and once you've got them in trance, you can look them in the eyes without them looking away. That's when you make the real connection. So with a little bit of practice, you can dispense with the passes and go straight to the gaze — you do have to be confident, though. This is the one that won't work unless you are confident, so make sure you practice all that has gone before until you are proficient at it all, before you try to work with gaze alone, because that "builds the muscles" you need, and instills confidence in what you are doing. That is very important. Now, it isn't very easy to describe the Gaze in words, because it is not a big, easily noticed movement... but when you get it right, you immediately see the difference in your victim's face, as their expression completely changes as they get totally

Enchantment

drawn into your gaze. At its very simplest, just do everything you did before, but all of it is projected through the gaze.

The "Evil Eye"

The evil eye, the Maloik, or Malocchio (Italian), is manipulation through gaze. The main difference is that in most cases, historically, the evil eye is not done deliberately. What happens with the evil eye, and I love its proper gypsy name, the Maloik, is that somebody is in a state of distress and dispassion, because life sucks, and when a dispassionate person gazes into the eyes of somebody else, especially if it's the eyes of a child, or a baby, they pass that dispassion onto them. So if you were severely depressed and just had given up, you could pass that onto somebody. It's one of those things when at the very end, when all else is failed, and your arch nemesis is gloating over you, you gaze dispassionately into their eyes, and curse them with the evil eye. That's when you use it deliberately. It's a bit like in the Harry Dresden books – "The Dresden Files", where they call it the Wizard's death curse. Well it is very similar, anyway. You wish your dispassion and despair upon them, and it's extraordinarily effective — that's why you'll see little old Italian ladies, when they see the Evil Eye, they make a warding

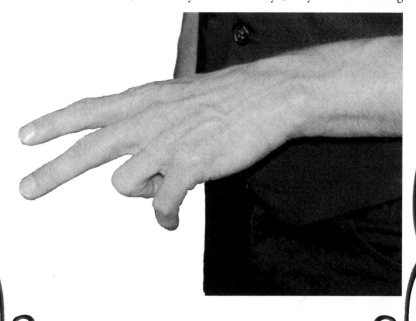

gesture, usually the index and middle finger of the left hand in a kind of inverted "peace" sign, angled down in the direction of the person who is the source of the evil eye, rotating their fingers as if winding the "thread" of the curse in order to prevent it attaching to anyone because that is a manipulating gesture. A lot of the hand gestures we use in ritual in different Witchcraft traditions are doing similar things, but with a religious/spiritual backing. So when you do your meditations, when you call in the quarters and you do the various signs, in the quarters, they are part of the same process. They are gestures. They are putting the 'fluence out there, you're just aiming it at the universe instead of a person.

Manipulating and Trance-Inducing Through Eye-Contact

The simplest way to do it, just with gaze, when you're first starting, is to visualize the passes you did in the last exercise. So you visualize the strokes or waves, and then you visualize the circling and then you visualize the drawing in. Then you just put the force of your focus into your gaze towards your victim. Feel almost a physical connection, and draw them in. You've got to be calm and, again, dispassionate, but without the despair; otherwise, that makes it the evil eye. So it really

Enchantment

is very, very simple, but you need to practice it a lot in order to get the hang of it. Give yourself a definite goal, of drawing the person towards you. So they fall or move towards you. You should start with a willing victim, then when you feel confident in your results, try it out on random people in the street. Remember, don't do anything harmful, but see if you can make people start coming towards you, then "let go" — they should almost immediately look a little puzzled, before shaking it off and going about their business.

When you practice on a friend, they should tell you that they are feeling it every bit as much as with the passes. It takes time and practice, and that is one of the reasons why I say that every piece of homework I give you, you have to keep doing all the time. It's not just so your homework list gets bigger and bigger and bigger, but because the results are cumulative. It is fun, so it shouldn't be too much of a chore.

Using the Gaze on Someone Who is Not Looking at You

So what do you do if a person you want to influence with gaze alone because they're too far away to touch, like the person standing in line in front of you – they aren't going to be looking at you, so what do you do?

Now, you could make them turn around and face you, but if you want them to not take that plate, having them turn around and face you is extra effort, and I'm lazy, don't know about you. I don't want to go to the effort of making them turn around, glaze, glare at them for a second, and then make them choose a different plate: that is way too much work. Luckily for us, we're not talking about physical vision with this technique. We're talking about essentially astral vision, for want of a better name. You see where I'm going with this? Astral vision, the subtle sight, has an interesting property – because there are no physical organs associated with astral sight, you're not limited to facing in one particular direction — astral vision is 360 degrees. It's one of the reasons why sometimes when you dream, you dream you're in your bedroom, but the bedroom door is on the wrong side of the room. This is because you perceive it multi-dimensionally, and you are perceiving it from all directions at once, so your brain is used to standard, forward-facing, stereoscopic vision, and sometimes it gets confused, and so it puts the door on the other side of the room.

So the door won't open when you go over there to open it, because the door's actually over on the other side, where it should be.

It takes a little bit of practice to get used to, but the same thing happens in astral projection. It is the second hardest thing about astral projection, apart from staying there once you get out for the first time. Doing these kind of exercises will very likely result in you developing the ability to astral project, and I can guarantee your very first successful astral projection will be "I'm out... oh, I'm back in". It's really annoying, and you won't be able to go out again 'til the next day at least, because that's just the way it works. When you slam back in, you'll end up with a headache, and then you have to let yourself relax again, usually with a good night's sleep, before you can try it again. Because the first time we get out, we've been trying hard for a long time, and we try too hard, so we sort of catapult out and the moment we realize we're out, we're back in again. It's really annoying. Likewise, the first thing that happens when you realize you're lucid dreaming, is that you wake up. Staying asleep takes practice, and staying out once you realize you're astral projecting takes practice for exactly the same reason.

Therefore you have to practice. It is the same with this. You're going to try too hard, and then you will have to relax, and then try it a little less hard next time, but because you can see 360 degrees with your astral vision, when somebody isn't facing you, their astral vision still sees you, subconsciously, and you lock gaze with that. The way I describe it to myself, because the idea of the eye contact is an emotional necessity for me, and it won't work for me without that eye contact, I make contact with their eyes through the back of their head. I visualize that I can see through their head, and there are their eyes, and for those of you who know my phobia about eyeballs, this is a very strange thing to be saying, but I see their eyes looking at me back through their head, and next thing you know, they're doing whatever you want them to do. So, once you've had a few successes from manipulating people from direct eye contact, try influencing a few people where you are not physically making eye contact. It should be obvious that you can, of course, do this from the side or from any other angle as well.

One of the students in the workshop pondered whether it would work "in reverse", where the victim was behind the manipulator. I

suggested that she try it, and she got a very good result, succeeding in getting her partner to reach out and touch her shoulder, which is what she was trying to influence them to do.

Another student described the feeling of doing this kind of manipulation as feeling like the prelude to a deity possession. Possession is where you allow a spirit or a deity to inhabit you, usually willingly, but it can happen spontaneously. When you are gazing on someone and you're making that connection, you're doing the same kind of soul connection that you would do with a deity, to enter a possession. We're kind of hardwired to go passive when that doorway gets opened, and as a consequence, you can take advantage of that. You are being like a god to them, but don't let it go to your head.

When you're influencing people against their will, you don't necessarily want them to know you're doing it. So if your practice partner thinks they just suddenly had an impulse to reach out and touch, or whatever you were trying to get them to do, then that's cool. That's how it's supposed to work.

"Gazing From Afar"

So, you've got the attention of the guy in line in front of you at the buffet, in order to make sure you get the dish you want, but what happens if you know somebody's going to be going down to the buffet, and they're going to hog all the shrimp, but they're in a different hotel room. How do you influence them? Well, the first thing you are likely to do is grab your crystal and use that, which is actually a perfectly logical way of doing it, but you can do this with the gaze, over a distance. If you know what they look like, you can "gaze" at them from anywhere on the planet, once you've got your confidence levels up. It's one of these things where it's got to be line of sight to start off with, then it's going to be within reach, and then it's going to be in the same room, then it's the same town, and so on and so forth. You're going to have to build up to it, but ultimately there are no distance limits to this.

Enchantment

Using Spoken Word

*T*here's really only one step further to go with influencing people, and it may seem like a step backwards, but you'll very soon see why it's a big step forward — using the spoken word. It is the power of the Voice, a bit like the "Bene Gesserit Voice" in the Dune novels. You will be able to do this, only without nice sound effects built into it, the nice echo, a bit of reverb, a bit of phasing, that they used in the movie... well, we don't have an astral sound effect kit to help us with that, but the really cool thing about when you use words to influence people, is you can influence more than one person at the same time. Perhaps not the best example, but it's one of the best-known examples, is the way Hitler influenced the people at the Nuremburg Rallies.

The Power of Words

Hitler was a master of this. It's how he got where he got, to everyone's deep chagrin. Words can be used on crowds, and it's exactly the same

Enchantment

technique as we've been using here, but obviously with a crowd of people, you can't focus your gaze on everyone at once because you'd go cross-eyed, and then you'd fall over. That's not really a very good way to influence people, unless you're going for the sympathy vote, though sometimes it's all you have, but it really is exactly the same technique. Hold a strong mental picture of what you desire, and send the thought out in a way, you visualize it as a ripple going out, touch everybody. That's the basics. You talk to get their attention. So they're receptive. If they're listening to you, they will "listen" to the energy that you're sending out, just as all my students listen to me in my workshops. As they listen, they passively pick up the signal, and here's the really cool part – they retransmit it. So you get an effect that is something like throwing a stone in a pond — you get the initial ripples, and then it hits other things and ripples from ripples, and you get this whole interference pattern going on, like the opening credits of classic Doctor Who. It amplifies and strengthens itself.

Directly Manipulating Groups or Crowds

This is where the group mind, or the mob intellect, comes in, and you take hold of that in both hands, and you manipulate it. It really is that simple, and the really cool thing is, what you're saying with your mouth doesn't have to be the message that you're giving out in the energy. Because they will hear the words you say, but they will react to the message in your energy. Once again, all the old rules apply. Phrase it positively. Don't send out a "don't go to the docks tonight", because they'll all go to the docks.

You can be really subtle with it. I mean a great example of this is the speech of Marc Antony at the funeral of Caesar. "I come to bury Caesar, not to praise him". Put the energy behind that and what do you get? "I come to bury Caesar — praise him!" That's how he turned the tide, and influenced the people of Rome. It is a masterful piece of oration, because it works on a magical level as well on a semantic level.

But you don't have to be a great orator. If you really want to seal the deal, that energy wave you're sending out, put some circular motion into it, so you actually draw the people closer. You're essentially doing the energetic equivalent of that gesture. You can get them eating out of your hand and listening to every word that you don't say.

There are classes available that teach you to embed messages in your words that can't be resisted, which are aimed at being used by sales reps, but they're using semantics and psychology, rather than enchantment. It's more like neuro-linguistic programming (NLP), which is very effective, but NLP ends with silence, and this doesn't. You can build up the energy, pull everyone into that moment of silence, and then put out one last wave of energy, and everyone is hooked like a fish. You've seen it happen – in the movies, at least. To be honest, any of you who have been to any of my workshops have been on the receiving end of this, because this is how I teach. That's what I'm doing in every class, every presentation. It's what I do when I teach workshops locally in Los Angeles. It's what I do when I teach workshops at PantheaCon. It's what I do when I'm trying to convince people to give me an iPad at work – that one actually worked really well, as did working to get a trip round the world — a world tour — which worked better than I could have ever expected. My boss basically said "yes, pack your bags and go now", and I had so many places to visit, I had to get someone else to cover some of them. So, as the saying goes, be careful what you wish for.

Now, this isn't something that's practical to really practice. It's just something that when you have an opportunity to try it, try it. You know, if you're a teacher, you'll have plenty of opportunity, or you get to talk to groups of people. Try it. Meeting at work, your turn to give a presentation, have them eating out of your hand. Really impress your boss, or really make him embarrass himself. That's almost better, but hopefully you can see where I'm going with that.

Well, that's basically it. That's what this book is all about. All the techniques that we've covered so far, the more you practice them, the less you'll have to do them. It's like I said at the very beginning, with the martial arts. You start off in your very first karate lesson, learning exaggerated movements, and by the time you've got your black belt, you're going through much simpler, fluid motions, barely moving at all. It becomes a flow rather than a movement, but you have to do the exaggerated movements to train your body, train your mind, train your soul... and train the energy. Then, bit by bit, as you become more confident, more practiced and more adept, the actual techniques fall away, leaving you with the pure manipulation. Until you come to a point, if you get really good at this, where you can just look at someone, or even just be aware of someone, and make them do what you want. From there, there is really no limit to where you can take this.

Enchantment

Glamour

So this is where we tie it all together. In the last chapter, we did all the cool exercises that were the actual meat of the sandwich, which is what everybody was doing this for in the first place, and I've heard various mutterings from those who participated in the workshops here in Los Angeles, and in the remote groups around the world, that they got some interesting results from practicing what I taught them. One example of the practical application of what was taught in the workshops, came from my friend Toni, who was having trouble with the agency she worked for:

"I was having trouble getting them to pay me a couple of weeks ago, because somebody in the payroll department decided that I only had one job, instead of the two that I actually have, and decided to put in just the single day job, instead of one for one day and the other for four days – just one day's pay for my whole week's salary, and I was not getting anyplace trying to get it fixed.

Enchantment

107

"So I started working on the manipulation, and I guess I worked on it a little bit hard because I not only got my paycheck, because I got money that one of the banks I have accounts with had been holding for me for 6 years, and every time I asked for it, they said no we don't have it, no we don't have it, no we don't have it. And the day that I started the manipulation, they cut the check. So I got the money from the bank we'd been waiting for six years to receive, my back pay from the payroll issue, and a check from a class action lawsuit we didn't even know we were part of."

Toni's result brings up an interesting point — don't be too specific about how you want your end goal. You might get an extra little surprise in the mail.

Creating an Illusion

Glamour is basically creating an illusion, and it can be a very subtle thing, where you just make somebody feel a little different about something, through to making them actually see and feel things, but we don't always have to go that far. The most important thing about creating a glamour is you need to develop a rapport with the person that you're placing the glamour on, because you need to basically get into their mind, and into their thought processes. Everything we've done up to now is part of that process, developing a rapport. So when you're doing your little manipulations that we did in the exercises, getting people to turn one way or another, giving them silent instructions, this is developing a rapport. As they respond to your incredibly magical abilities, you very quickly get to a point where you can start to have a greater influence on them. Every successful step you take with a person gives you more power over them, basically. You can put a glamour on somebody whether they're standing in front of you or whether they're in a different country. It doesn't matter where they are. If you know what they look like and you've established a rapport with them, you can put the glamour on them wherever they are, which is where the real fun begins. You start off putting the glamour on by changing their mood, making them feel happy, or warm and cozy, or secure. Or if you're maleficent, make them feel frightened, make them feel uncertain, make them feel uncomfortable. You know, like a politician, like the government, or anybody in any position of authority these days, it seems. Now, obviously you should try and pick something that's appropriate to where you're heading. If you're going to want somebody to fall in love with you, and that was an example not a suggestion –I don't recommend doing that — you do not want to start off giving them the screaming heebie-jeebies, because you're kind of sending them in the wrong direction; i.e., running for the hills. It is a bit difficult to get a warm embrace thrown in there somewhere, if they're too busy packing for their survival shelter. So, work with appropriate things, but just start small, start with the feelings.

Then, you want to fine tune that feeling that you want them to have as part of the final glamour. There's usually an object to the glamour. You're either putting a glamour on them so they see things differently, and it affects them or the way they see you, or the way they see another person or another thing. For example, this is something I did when I was a kid. I got change back from my lunch money at school when I was about 7, and I thought I was the richest kid on the block, because I had cash in my hand. It didn't occur to me that my mother would want it back, but that's another story. So I came out of school at the end of the school day, and my dad was waiting to walk me home, but I didn't want to go home, I wanted to go to the toy store up the road, and I guess I had something of an ability for glamour, even at the age of seven because I managed to convince him that I wasn't me and walked right past him without him recognizing me. He'd only known me for 7 years at that point, but he totally missed the fact that I walked right past him. That I went and spent the money on toys and candy, and got into a lot of trouble when I got home for upsetting my father and for spending the money that I was supposed to give back to my mother. It was because we had a day off that week. I mean we're talking like 15 pence, but it was a lot of money when you were seven. It was enough for a bunch of Black Jack chews, you could get 8 of them for a penny back then, and then you could buy a water pistol for 5 pennies, and that was apparently incentive enough for me to manifest my inner Harry Potter!

So you start to turn the feelings that you've been working on around a little bit and have them apply that feeling in connection with the thing you want to place the glamour on, whether it's them, you, or someone or something else. So you've gotten pretty good – and this is

Enchantment

a lot easier to do, obviously, when they're physically present because you can see the results. You are pretty much running on assumptions when you're doing it from a distance. So start off easy, and deal with

somebody face to face, I guarantee it'll work better for you that way, and it does take practice. There aren't going to be any exercises for this stage, because it is simply a matter of applying the directions that have been already given, but so you basically want to get them to see the object of the glamour the way you want them to see it. Now this doesn't have to be sort of rainbows and unicorns, or some kind of psychedelic Sgt. Pepper's Lonely Hearts Club Band surrealist imagery, because that takes quite a bit of work. Normally when you do a glamour, it's something subtle. Perhaps you want to make that cute blond at the office think you look a little bit more handsome than you really do

— that's actually really easy to do, because when you're attracted to somebody, you see them as more attractive, and so as part of the process of getting them to fancy you, that comes with the territory. So you don't have to try too hard for that one, once you got stage one down.

If you're trying to conceal something or make somebody look like somebody else, you have to work a little harder, and it's going to take a little more practice to get to that point, but you can do it. By now, you will have seen and experienced some pretty cool things, if you have been working through the exercises I have given. An important aspect of learning to do this, is that it proves that magick isn't just psychology — this stuff does really work; it's just a matter of practicing it and keeping at it. It's like riding a unicycle. Once you've got the hang of it, it's easy, but if you stop doing it, you're going to lose the knack and have to start again to get yourself back into it. So remember that, it is a good excuse to manipulate people left, right and center.

Finally, you complete the glamour by commanding that the object is as you wish it to be. The basic idea here is, and we'll be talking about this a bit more later, because it applies to the next step, is that, once you've got them in the palm of your hand, you issue commands. You tell them what you want them to see or do, pure and simple, and you'll be pleased to know that if you're doing it from a distance, your trusty crystal can help. There's a slight variation on the technique with the crystal you can use. Some people find it works better for this, and some people prefer to use the technique given earlier in the book, so try it and see, and if you like the other one better, go back to using that, but you basically hold your crystal ball or whatever crystal you've ended up with, as if it's the eyepiece of a telescope, and you hold it up a few inches from your eye, so you can look through it. Then, you do exactly the same process, but you imagine that the "telescope" is this huge tube that sort of wends its way over to wherever the person is, and so you can see them. So, you do all the visualizing as if you're looking at them through a psychic telescope. It gives you a visual image of being connected with them, and once you've got that image nice and clear, you basically deal with them as if you were standing next to them. So the rest of it is just the same as working on somebody who's in your presence.

One of the workshop attendees said that she has put a glamour on the person interviewing her for a job, so that they would see her as the perfect person for the position. I've done that frequently with job interviews as well. I spent many years working as a software programmer, and I developed a habit of when I wanted to learn something new, I would find someone who was hiring for a position doing that thing, go to the interview and convince them I could do that thing, and then once I got the job, figuring out how the hell to do that thing. Having a deadline gives you an incentive, and I'm basically a lazy person, as a lot of us are. Having that deadline made me get up off my backside, buy some books and learn to do it. Otherwise, I just sat talking around procrastinating. You could almost say I put a glamour on myself as well.

Persuasion

Closely connected with glamour, using many of the same techniques and energies, persuasion is probably actually the thing you're going to use more often, because glamour in a way is the superstar of magical manipulation, and it's kind of fun, but how many times do you need somebody to think you're their cousin? Unless your name is Uther Pendragon, and you want to pretend to be Igraine's husband, for nefarious and naughty purposes, you're probably not going to use glamour a lot in all honesty. Well, you will to play with, but there won't be many serious applications, although it's a really good psychic workout. This is a really good day at the gym for your magical muscles.

Persuasion means getting your own way, and takes less effort, less energy, and is a much more practical technique to use in your everyday life. So I heartily recommend that you persuade up one side and down the other, because that's good exercise, too. It's basically the same thing except you're not trying to make them see something that isn't there. Essentially, persuasion is a combination of putting a bit of a mild glamour on them so you change how they feel a little, and then giving them commands. It is really useful for getting somebody to agree to do something that they wouldn't normally agree to do, or to believe something that they wouldn't normally believe. It is great way of putting across a lie — white lies, of course, because we're all good people, aren't we? What we're talking about is "these are not the Droids you're looking for". The really cool thing is you can persuade someone in advance. You don't have to do it while you're physically present, because you can do it beforehand. Say you're going for a job interview, or you're doing a sales pitch, or you've got a meeting at work, and you need to focus on those events, because they're not things you can just sort of sleepwalk through. So you do your persuading before you get there. You basically visualize the meeting or the interview, or whatever, and you do it strongly and clearly as you can, and once you've got the visualization there nice and clear, you then act, behave as if the person is actually physically in the room with you, or the meeting is actually going on in the room with you right now. You usually spend about 10 minutes doing that, and it's going to be hard to focus for 10 minutes. You're going to get 2, 3 minutes tops at the beginning, but aim for 10 minutes, because by the time you can do 10 minutes, you're going to get guaranteed results, but so, you know, it's just building those muscles up again.

You are basically going to visualize the meeting or the interview going on the way you expect it to, but you hold in your mind the thought of what it is you want to happen. This usually works best if, obviously, you remember to phrase everything in positive terms, because the universe doesn't know the word no. It usually works best if you phrase it in the first person singular. If you want somebody to sign that contract, and you use the phrase "you will sign that contract...", what happens is, they think, "I feel like somebody's trying to compel me. Oh, I better not do this because otherwise there'll be hell to pay". It's essentially self-defeating; you can force it, but one of you is going to have a mental hernia over it, because there's going to be a struggle involved, which means it is going to take way more effort than it needs to.

What you want to do is you want to impel them, and so instead of saying "you will sign that contract", you say "I'm going to sign that contract", as if you're thinking the words for them. Get what I mean? So then when that idea pops into their head, they think "I've just had an idea. How unusual!"

The other thing you can do, as well as saying "I'm going to sign that contract" – and you want to "say it" in a positive and confident manner — is you want to use impelling words. Now, the cunning linguists amongst us all know that impelling words are words that draw you in. You start the sentence with a word like "well", as in "well, you know, I'm going to sign that contract". It draws you in, gets you involved, and you know, if you're trying to get that appointment to see somebody who

Enchantment

113

just nobody gets to see, the words you can say to them is "well, I'm going to have you come back here at 1 o'clock". So "well" is the easiest one to use, so just use it. My favorite use of this is for persuading guests who outstay their welcome... "well, I'm going to be going now".

So remember, keep using positive statements. If you want someone to get healthy, don't use the impelling phrase, "well, I'm going to lose weight" – because they'll start stuffing. Use the "well, it's time to get healthy". Actually, you can use that on yourself as well, because one of the people you can persuade with this technique, is you.

Invoking Desire

Then there's invoking desire. Now this isn't just for sex — I know, you're all looking disappointed now. You can get sexual desire out of this if you're really unethical. It is unethical, unless you know they really want it, and they're just playing hard to get, though it is almost impossible to be certain of that, but you can use it to draw someone to you. Say you want a business partner, say you want somebody to hang out with but, you know, they've already got someone to hang out with and they don't really notice you that much. Or maybe we're not talking about a specific person. You've just moved to a new city, and you want to find out where all the good Pagans are... well, not where all the good Pagans are, where all the fun Pagans are. They're not necessarily the same thing. Or maybe you've just opened a new store and you want to draw some customers in, or you got a new job at a store and you want to draw customers in so your new boss can see how wonderful you are. Well, this is how you do it. Each day, concentrate for a few minutes — 2-3 minutes up to 10 minutes, if you can develop the muscles for it — on who or what you wish to draw to you, and just let your thoughts go out in waves. Send them out to the universe. They don't have to be aimed at a specific person or type of person, you don't have to aim, "well, I know most of the Pagans live over in that part of town, so I'm going to push it out that way". No, just send it out like ripples in a pond. You are the stone – plop, ripples, and as I said, you can use it to draw customers, draw students, draw lovers, draw partners... you can use it to create trust, and the really cool thing is that one of the ways this works is that it's one of these "like attracts like" things. You send out the vibration that you want to draw back in. So if you want friendly camaraderie and company, the energy you're putting out is friendliness, camaraderie and being good company, and you put that into a simple phrase like "this is the place to find fun". "This is the place to find love".

Because what happens is that wave of information, energy, vibe, juju, mojo, whatever you want to call it, wafts out in all directions, and when it connects with minds, the ones that are conducive pick up on it and they bounce it back. So it is the same thing when we're talking about influencing a bunch of people when you're talking to a group, like when teaching a class. When people are receptive, and they pick it up, because of the nature of the way this works, it's going to work, it's going to affect the people who match that frequency. They then start transmitting it, too, so it's like social networking. It is not just the decision that "I'll come round to Peter's place. It's a great place to hang out and talk to Pagans" but they're transmitting that and saying, "I'm going out, I'm going to a place where it's great to hang around and have fun and talk with Pagans. Why don't you come, too". In a sense, it becomes this whole complex pattern of ripples going out in all different directions, like the ripples bounce off the edge of the pond or anything else in the water, and each other, before coming back in a complex interference pattern, and it gets amplified along the way.

So persuasion doesn't have to be aimed at a person; when you're doing it to draw people in, you can just throw it out at the universe. In fact, in a lot of cases, you find that not being too specific works better. I mean, Toni, who had the issue with her pay, was initially trying really hard to resolve it, trying to manipulate the person who writes the checks, and it wasn't working. She said to the world in general "why isn't this working? I'm trying really hard at this person, I'm sure they're the right person". My response when she told me was, "well, don't be so specific. Sometimes if you just put up to the universe I want more money, it works better because it leaves the universe to find the way that works". Maybe that person doesn't have the authority to decide to write an extra check. By leaving it open, you open up the possibility that somebody else could make that decision, and as we saw, three other people made that decision. I still haven't seen my commission yet, though....

Another student asked me about working on inanimate objects. She is a big fan of antiques, and sometimes she'd see something she

Enchantment

absolutely had to own, but couldn't afford right them. She wanted to know if enchantment could prevent someone else from buying it.

Well, there's a couple of ways you can do that. You can work on a glamour on the object so that anybody who sees it is disinterested, which is going to be more like the reverse of drawing people to you. In this instance, you're pushing people away. It's the same idea that we discussed earlier, but when people see that thing they go "meh", and walk past, or maybe just not even see it, which is easier.

The other option, which may be more practical, is that whoever else is in the store with the thing that you want, put a glamour on them, that they've already put it aside for you. Do something like the interview thing — walk through going there and buying it right now, so that they believe, as far as they're concerned, that it is sold. So when people ask for it, they say "oh, no, sorry, that's sold", and then you walk in three days later, when you've finally got the money together, and it's still there. The clerk says "oh, yes, I've got your thing here". It can actually happen: the first time you ever walk in a store – you've walked past it, looked in the window, and seen something you wanted, and did the glamour. Three days later you walked in, crossing the threshold for the first time, and the clerk behind the counter looks up at you and says "oh, yes, I've got your item here. That will be X". It's really cool. I actually had that happen – there's a rock shop in Burbank — "Rocks and Runes", off Magnolia Boulevard, a really cool store — and I walked in there, the very first time I'd actually walked in there, looking for moldavite, and as I walked in, and the lady said, "oh, yes, I remember from when you were here 3 days ago, and I put some aside for you". So, it really does work that well. The trouble is, I get distracted with other things, too many things to keep it up, otherwise, I'd have everything by now.

Protecting Yourself

So what do you do when someone else is trying to do this to you?

Preventing Others From Placing a Glamour on You

Protecting yourself is really easy. If you feel somebody putting the glamour or the 'fluence, or any of this, on you — and believe me you will feel it because now you're doing it, you'll recognize it when it comes back at you — you just push back. It's as simple as that. If you feel a glamour coming on you – "oh, I feel glamorous all of a sudden" – just put a glamour back, a "leave me alone" glamour. Or "if you don't leave me alone you're going to be in a hole in my backyard". You don't actually have to do it, and you're not putting it in writing, so they can't get you for the threat. If somebody tries to persuade you, you persuade

Enchantment

them back. If somebody tries to make you turn left at Albuquerque, you say screw you, I'm turning right. When you recognize it, it's actually pretty easy to ignore. As I said, you have probably noticed how easy every one of these exercises has been, because it's very gentle. It's very subtle. It's because we're hard-wired to be an easy pushover, until we know it's happening, and all it takes to stop any of this from happening is for you to realize it is happening, and say no. That's the one time the universe does understand the word no. It'll stop it dead in most cases, unless they're really good, and then you have to push back properly.

Patron Deities and Guardian Spirits

There's another way you can protect yourself from being under the influence of others, and this is the one part of this whole process where we talk about religion or spirituality. Because you can use your guardian angel, your guardian spirit, your patron deity, whoever you work with on the "other side", to set up as a watchman, to watch your back. Because, let's be honest, when you're doing this to someone else, you are actually quite open, and you're really fairly unprotected, so this is where you pull in your tradition, your spirituality, your other magical practices, to have somebody stand guard over you while you do it, because in order to put that energy out there, you have to open the doors. It's a bit like you can't fire the photon torpedoes if the shields are up. You have to drop shields, fire the torpedoes, and if you like, your patron spirit or guardian spirit is Worf at the tactical station, ready with the phasers.

So it's a good idea. This is the part where I reveal that all of it actually works better if you put it into your spiritual framework and your regular spiritual practice. I mean you've been doing this as an exercise just sitting there, pure thought energy and pure you, playing with your crystal, and playing with manipulations, right? Now put that into one of your rituals, or into a spell crafting. All of the focus and the energy and the power of the tradition you work, added to what you're already doing here. That's why I haven't done any of that up until this point, because it is the final ingredient. Once you get good at it in the generic form presented in this book, put it into your magical, regular magical practice, and suddenly ka-boom — you just upped the caliber of your psychic guns significantly, but I'm not going to tell you how to do that because it's your path. You know what your spiritual path is about, what your rituals, what your spells, what your gods and what-have-you are all about, so you add that ingredient yourself. That's why I stuck to pure technique. Of course, you can actually have a person, a partner, stand guard for you as well. If you're doing it by yourself, you definitely want someone from Upstairs or Downstairs, or across the Universe, to do it for you.

You can also use this technique pro-actively for protection, because you can use the persuasion on an area, room, or space. Say you just moved into a new house, and you love the house, it's great for work, it's got nice rooms and everything, but there's a part of the house — maybe one of the bedrooms — that just feels icky, because somebody lived there before and did something stupid or nasty. So it's just "ugh, I get the heebie-jeebies", every time you walk in there. Well, you can put a glamour on the room. You can persuade the room to become more positive by using these exact techniques – focus them on the room instead of a person, and of course, for your own self-improvement and self-edification, and sometimes self-entertainment, you can use them on yourself.

Conclusion
What Can We Do With All This?

So, what all can we do with all this? Where do we go from here? Well, first and foremost, you have the responsibility as magical practitioners to use this ethically — sorry, guys — no matter how much you want to glamour somebody into pulp from time to time. We all have a list of people, let's be honest, who we'd like to make go away. Generally speaking, it's not ethical to do so. If you misuse this, it's going to come back at you — not because of any three-fold law, not because of any Karmic debt – it is because those ripples hit the side and they bounce back, and you want what comes back at you to be positive. So think about what you're doing, and make sure that what you're doing isn't going to bounce back on you and cause you trouble.

Also, no matter how big and strong and good at this stuff you are, sooner or later, you'll find somebody who's better, and if you're doing the bad stuff, they're going to take you and spank your behind, magically speaking, which might be fun in that club you go to on a

Friday night, but not so much fun when some adept in some magical order decides to take it upon himself to give you a lesson in ethics. So do good things. Don't do anything to anybody that you would be upset about somebody doing to you, and you should be OK. But sometimes it's right to mete out some justice, but make sure you're willing to pay the coin. I don't recommend hurting people under any circumstances, but you know, defense of the nation, defense of the family — if there's a good, valid reason for those, you take good care of it.

Healing and Therapy

You can use these techniques for healing and therapy; however, the usual caveat applies. Don't mess with things you don't understand. You can do more harm than good if you try to heal somebody if you don't really know what's wrong with them, or if you do something that conflicts with any other treatment they're having. You know, luckily there aren't any sort of contra-indications in the pharmacists' books for this stuff, so it's not like herbal medicine, where if you give someone St. John's Wort, and they're on the wrong medication from their doctor, you're going to put them in a world of hurt: but if somebody has untreated schizophrenia, or untreated depression, or untreated something nasty going on in their heads, and you start putting a glamour on them, you're going to make them worse. So if you try and heal them of something else — such as they're just having a bad time, and you want to cheer them up — but there's this underlying mental condition, and you throw a glamour in there, put them into a world of illusion –you might as well just give them acid for all the good you're going to do them. Acid could be fun, but there are certain people who shouldn't take it because they're already halfway there, and they may never come back if you give it to them, so be careful and thoughtful about what you're doing. Somebody has a broken leg, you can put the 'fluence on them and do use the persuasion to help them heal faster, help bone mend faster — that works. That's one of the reasons why last year when I was in hospital with my leg twice the normal size, and festering with god knows what hanging out of it, I was in hospital for 3 days where everybody else I know who has been in that position was in for 3 weeks or longer. Because the combination of my own efforts, once I was feeling up to it, and everyone around me putting juju into me big time, accelerated the healing process; and they also got in those thwaps up the side of the head for letting myself get into that situation as well so fair play to them.

Creating Opportunities

Obviously you can create opportunities: that job interview, or an interview with the media, maybe, if you want to become the official spokesperson for your area on something. Put the 'fluence on to make sure you're the one they call. You can use it charitably to make a difference if there's a really good fundraiser going on, but you really haven't got a lot of money to spare, or you haven't got time to spare, but you can put the 'fluence out to encourage everyone else to go. That's a fairly good thing to do — make people go spend their money, and you can be smug and satisfied without having spent any yourself.

Accelerated Learning

You can, as I've already mentioned, use this on yourself. You can use it to accelerate your own learning. If you need to learn something for an exam, or you need to learn a skill, put the 'fluence on yourself to maximize your learning process. You can do it to someone else as well. If your kid's got an exam, you can put the 'fluence on them, if you think they're not trying hard enough, turn them around. Make sure you do it ethically, though, but you can do all of this on yourself to improve yourself.

We're going to be getting back into our eating healthy and exercising regime at long last. We've finally got to a point where we're ready to do it, and one of the things I'm going to be doing is I'm going to be putting the 'fluence on me to stop being a lazy bugger, so I will get up in the morning and go for that walk, regardless of whether my knees are aching, or my back's aching, because the walk will help the ache. It's just that at 5:30 in the morning, it's very easy to say, "as long as I do it 3 times a week", once or twice, you can get away with that, but the 3rd time, it's just wrong. So I'm going to 'fluence myself, and I'm sure that Linda wouldn't have said anything, but she's going to 'fluence me, too, because she wants me to get out there and walk as well. So, I wouldn't be surprised if there are definitely going to be some changes — I expect us all to be fighting fit and wealthy and well-employed and, and really influential people by the end of the year because we're all going to be so good at this.

Enchantment

Cursing and Harmful Manipulation

Last but not least – this is a use for this stuff I heartily recommend you don't do — but just as knowledge of herbal medicine enables you to heal or harm, you can use all of these techniques to curse. I'm sure you can see exactly how that works, so I'm not going to spell it out for you. Please don't, because it's not nice, and you know, the whole ethics thing comes in. So although sometimes there's a damn good reason to curse — not because you don't like the additions to your chant that people are using, like certain people have done recently — there's often better reasons not to.

It can be tempting to just doing bad things to mess with people's heads, and you can actually be a very malicious person with this stuff, but as I said, it's your responsibility to use it wisely. Sometimes there may be a legitimate reason to pull out the nasties, but 99.9% of the time it's just not worth it, because you'll end up poking yourself in the eye every bit as much as you poke the other person in the eye. So don't do it.

At the end of the workshops, one of the participants asked, "so you've got someone doing some glamour on you, and you suspect they're not as ethical as you are, and it might be some bad stuff — when you push it back, does that go back to them, or does it just go away?"

The answer is that it depends on how you push, really. One of my favorite forms of psychic self-defense is the old mirror trick, where you put a mirror ball around yourself so that whatever's being thrown at you gets bounced back at the sender. I think it's perfectly, perfectly legitimate to shoot somebody with their own arrow if they're trying to shoot you.

Peter Paddon

Index

Peter Paddon

Enchantment

N

O

P

Enchantment

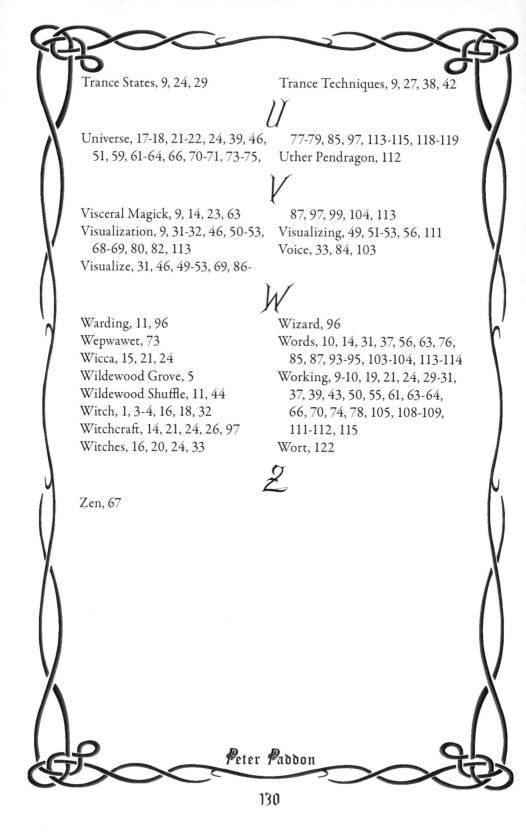

About the Author

Peter is a Brit of Welsh ancestry who lives in Los Angeles with his wife Linda, where he is Magister of the Y Ffordd Wen Tradition of the Cunning Arts. Aside from being an author, Peter also created the Craftwise series of spellcasting DVDs, and is the host of the Crooked Path podcast. A regular presenter at PantheaCon (the largest Pagan event on the West Coast), Peter also teaches workshops across the US, as well as globally via live streaming video.

Having many years of experience in various forms of Occult Studies, including Alexandrian Wicca, the Egyptian Mysteries, Rosicrucianism and Enochian magick, Peter finally found what he had been looking for all his life in the two Traditional Covens he became a member of in the US. The first was the Roebuck (1734, Clan of Tubal Cain), under Ann and Dave Finnin, and the second was Wildewood Grove (Welsh Celtic Tradition), under its Mistress, Raven Womack.

Enchantment

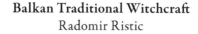

Magickal Works from Pendraig Publishing

Balkan Traditional Witchcraft
Radomir Ristic

Buckland's Domino Divinaton
*Fortune-Telling with Döminös
and the Games of Döminös*
Raymond Buckland

Buckland's Practical Color Magick
Raymond Buckland

Hedge-Rider
Witches and the Underworld
Eric De Vries

Magical Rites from the Crystal Well
The Classic Book for Witches and Pagans
Ed Fitch

Masks of the Muse
*Building a relationship
with the Goddess of the West*
Veronica Cummer

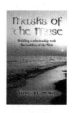

Mastering the Mystical Heptarchy
Scott Stenwick

Scottish Herbs and Fairy Lore
Ellen Evert Hopman

Sorgitzak: Old Forest Craft
*Stories and messages
from the gods of Old Europe*
Veronica Cummer

Fiction Novels *From Pendraig Publishing*

PENDRAIG   **PENDRAIG**

Arcana by Scott Stenwick
The Tale of Tyrfing by Sokarjo Stormwillow
The Wrath of Amun by Claudia Dillaire
Golden Illuminati by Raymond Buckland
Ragnarok Rising The Awakening by D.A. Roberts

The Demon's Apprentice Series by Ben Reeder
The Demon's Apprentice *Book 1*
The Page of Swords *Book II*

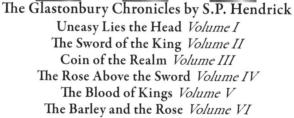

The Glastonbury Chronicles by S.P. Hendrick
Uneasy Lies the Head *Volume I*
The Sword of the King *Volume II*
Coin of the Realm *Volume III*
The Rose Above the Sword *Volume IV*
The Blood of Kings *Volume V*
The Barley and the Rose *Volume VI*

Tales of the Dearg-Sidhe by S.P. Hendrick
Son of Air and Darkness *Volume I*
Great Queen's Hound *Volume II*
The Pale Mare's Fosterling *Volume III*

Made in the USA
San Bernardino, CA
06 July 2018